It is impossible to say what leaving home means for everyone as each person's experiences are so different. For me, personally, it meant independence, self-worth and a sense of achievement. It's been two years since I left home and only now have I reached the point where I feel comfortable with my life. I went through a lot of emotional stress to get where I am today and I would never tell anyone that leaving home is necessarily the easiest option.

I was thrown out when I was 16 years of age because I wasn't getting on with my mum . . .

GW00685602

Jane Cassidy was the News Editor of *The Big Issue* for two and a half years, and continues to write for *The Big Issue* as a freelancer, as well as for several newspapers and magazines. She is also currently involved in work for BBC television and Channel 4. She lives in London.

Street Life

Young Women Write about Being Homeless

Jane Cassidy, editor

Livewire
from The Women's Press

First published by Livewire Books, The Women's Press Ltd, 1999
A member of the Namara Group
34 Great Sutton Street, London EC1V 0LQ

Collection copyright © Jane Cassidy 1999

The copyright in each of the pieces in this collection remains with the
original copyright holder.

The right of Jane Cassidy and the contributors to be identified as the
joint-authors of this work has been asserted by them in accordance with
the Copyright, Designs and Patents Act 1988.

British Library Cataloguing-in-Publication Data
A catalogue record for this book is available from the British Library.

This book is sold subject to the condition that it shall not, by way of trade
or otherwise, be lent, re-sold, hired out, or otherwise circulated without
the Publisher's prior consent in any form of binding or cover other than
that in which it is published and without a similar condition including
this condition being imposed on the subsequent purchaser.

ISBN 0 7043 4968 X

Typeset in 12/14pt Bembo by FSH Ltd, London
Printed and bound in Great Britain by Cox & Wyman Ltd,
Reading, Berkshire

Introduction

One story I was sent for this book was written on very dog-eared stained pieces of paper. The rips and the marks bore testimony to the writer's determination to tell her story. She was homeless, sleeping in car parks and derelict buildings; sheltering in shop doorways for much of her time, living from day to day. Her pen and scraps of paper were with her constantly, hidden inside her coat everywhere she went.

When you are homeless, the small details that many of us take for granted can become huge worries. While for some of us, the biggest decision of the day is what to have for lunch, others are agonising over where they will find the money for their next meal or somewhere safe to bed down for the night. When you are homeless, these concerns are enough to take up all your waking hours and it is hard to concentrate on planning further than one day ahead, let alone take the time to write about your experiences.

The women who contributed to this book were so eager to communicate their thoughts to others, to show what homelessness is really like, they took time out from sorting out basic survival needs, such as finding a roof over their heads, in order to tell their stories. Several of them felt they had to change their names because they were worried their families might read the book and recognise the descriptions of difficult and distressing situations. Some changed their names because they did not want to upset relatives they still care about; others because they were afraid of reprisals. So, family problems emerge as a big reason why many young women end up being homeless, rather than staying in a dangerous or unhappy environment.

Some writers felt they had gained confidence by becoming independent and leading lifestyles other than the ones mapped out for them by their cultures or families. But no one claimed life as a homeless person was easy. Homelessness isn't just sleeping on the streets or living rough. Being homeless means living without the security and comfort of permanent housing. It means living with constant uncertainty, a lack of privacy, an inability to relax, chill out and plan for the future. Having no address means it is difficult to find work, get access to health care, contraception, help during pregnancy, education or benefits. For some young women it means 'sofa surfing' at friends' houses because they have been thrown out of home or have left after an argument. It can mean staying in a bed and breakfast hotel, or in a hostel, which may have very strict rules about when you can come and go.

Some homeless people who are living in B&Bs or hostels are forced to leave their rooms early in the morning and cannot return until the evening. When you don't have any money or anywhere to go during the day, it can lead to intense boredom, loneliness, feelings of worthlessness, and depression. These feelings leave you vulnerable to the type of person who will pretend to help you in order to get what they want. Many homeless people find themselves being offered alcohol or drugs to dull the emotional pain, by people who then try to talk them into dangerous ways of making money, such as prostitution, theft, or drug dealing. Record numbers of young women are ending up homeless today, but the limited help available to them is often not tailored to their needs.

The aim of this book is certainly not to advocate homelessness as an attractive option to young women in trouble. In fact, the stories contained in this collection reveal just how hard it is to live as a homeless person. There are alternatives. The book ends with a help list for anyone who may be having similar problems to the ones described, with the names of groups you can contact for help and guidance. What this book does advocate is an understanding both of what leads someone to become homeless, and what life is really like on the streets.

The young women in this collection are all very aware of the misconceptions about homelessness and they are adamant that communication is the key to breaking down barriers. They know from their own experience that once people in the outside world see beyond the label and recognise them as individuals with their own histories and hopes, then they will begin to look differently on the people they meet as part of their everyday lives.

I would like to thank *The Big Issue*, particularly Neil Ansell; Erika Curren, Gill Price, Jean Willoughby, the staff at Centrepoint, Cecil House and London Connection; and all the contributors who gave their help and time to this book.

In Search of a Little Lost Love

Laura, 18

I firmly believe that age is not determined by years, but is a state of mind, a part of your individual character. It is an acquired quality, developed and variable according to one's life experiences and factors such as personal insight, a conscious awareness of the world, and an open attitude towards change. In essence, age is not something physical, but is a mental approach reflecting one's life and how it is led. My age in years is 18 and a half, but in mind?

Until recently my daily life was a roller-coaster travelling faster and faster downhill. Much of my time was spent on the streets: in prostitution, working them; in addiction, the never-ending search for drugs; and in living, the many days and nights lost to drug-induced insanity, homelessness, and the constant fear of returning to established accommodation.

★

I was born in 1980 to a single woman, the result of a brief fling. My father was not aware of my conception and, despite years of searching, to this day does not know of my existence. My mother was a lonely person, having lost her parents as a teenager. She lived by herself, had few friends, a poor social life, and her intellectual capacity never has been, and never will be, fulfilled.

The circumstances surrounding my birth still remain much of a mystery, but when I was born, my mother found through me all the things that were missing from her life. Security, a sense of belonging, a permanent home, a purpose, a friend, a family. Although I believe that she wanted to give me a good start in life, I am unable to explain what went wrong.

We had little money and few possessions, but living in a small country town beside the sea meant that keeping busy wasn't hard. There was always an interesting walk, whatever the weather, and plenty of time for learning new skills: games, reading, and writing. I could read fluently by the age of three. To save electricity when money was short, we often cooked foil-wrapped potatoes in the glowing embers beneath the fire. They were the best-tasting jacket potatoes ever! However, despite the good times – and there were good times – I have never loved my mother, or even come close to liking her. To the outside world I seemed a well brought-up, loved child; part of a normal family, really. But some of the lessons I learned were not so ordinary. Or, perhaps I should say, *shouldn't* be so ordinary.

I must have been about three when it started. The fear remains as clear as crystal in my memory, imprinted in every fold of my body. The overwhelming anxiety and terror I experienced after going to bed still haunt me now. So do the images of a man at my door. I always slept with my back pressed against the wall, relentlessly watching the door in anticipation of the slightest movement; arms tucked beneath the duvet, which I wrapped tightly about my neck. Sometimes, I would wake during the night, trembling in terror. The sound of heavy breathing rose from the floor, heavier than my own small breath. Fear never did allow me to sit up and look over the side of the bed.

Throughout my childhood years, both my mother and her partner (who moved in when I was six) used me like a piece of meat. The maternal love my mother should have offered was exchanged for domination and abuse. The authorities were far from oblivious but seemed to ignore the evidence. Their handling of my case was later the subject of negligence proceedings. Social services were criticised and threatened with a public enquiry by a high court judge. However, this ruling came too late to prevent the devastating consequences of my childhood. Many years of abuse, beatings and bullying, totally exhausted my somewhat fragile will to survive and destroyed my social skills and self-esteem. It sounds extreme, but I was ready to kill or be killed.

On 20 December 1993, I was taken into local authority care and placed in a foster home. This was the first of 19 moves during my 4 years in care, due to a shortage of long-term carers. The opportunity of escaping my past and living a normal life with an ordinary family had been a life-long dream. But my new foster parents were less than caring and the family made no attempt to welcome or include me. Lack of self-confidence soon left me isolated and confined to my room whilst in the house. The floundering, minuscule amount of spirit I had left ebbed still further away.

Six months later, however, the opportunity of a lifetime arose. I got a job with a reputable theatre company, caring for one of the performers – Doris, the horse – and spent eight blissful weeks, travelling and performing with some of the most easy-going, caring people I've ever met. Through theatre, acting and dance, I found a channel that enabled me to liberate myself from some of the grief that had remained buried for so long.

Part way through the tour, a new foster placement was arranged and I settled in during a weekend break. Things should have been looking up, but inside I felt more desperate than ever. My long-existent eating problems began to grasp hold again. Secretly, I sneaked food upstairs and, once hidden in my bedroom, would cram vast quantities into my mouth. After the initial relief, I was plagued by feelings of guilt, disgust and despair. So I dieted. And these diets took the form of month-long starvations, during which even water made me feel bloated, panicky and out of control. The strain of my eating habits put pressure on the foster placement and was the ultimate cause of its breakdown.

Then, I won a place at a specialised theatre college to study physical theatre, movement techniques, acrobatics, dance and music. At 15, I was by far the youngest student. A new placement was found within travelling distance of the course. However, it proved to be a disaster and fell apart at the beginning, only serving to escalate my already precarious eating disorder.

Every day revolved around my obsession with food.

Shopping became a ritual, checking the calorie content of every edible product displayed on the shelves. Items such as fruit that had no definite calorie value were far too risky and therefore forbidden, as was everything containing more than 100 calories per 100 grams. These restrictions meant that through fanatical exercise, laxative abuse, bingeing, throwing up, purging and calorie counting, I became increasingly unwell. My inner 'dictator', the controlling voice forever present in my mind, criticised my every thought and action. To the outside world, I was an ambitious, independent teenager. Inside I was a desperate, hurt and frightened child.

My next move occurred exactly two years to the day after I moved into care. This move gave me what I had been searching for: a home and family, love, patience, understanding, and the safety to release all the years of emotion stored up inside me. In my foster mum, Barbara, I found the mother I always wanted but never had. Wherever she went, fun and laughter followed. Her son, James, told his colleagues in London that he was going home to meet his 'new little sister'.

From the beginning, I fitted in, belonged. For the first time in my life I felt safe and was able to begin the process of learning how to trust. Yet it was this very salvation which activated a trigger, annihilating all my protective barriers, tumbling me deeper into the realms of self-destruction. I started cutting my body, mutilating it, wanting it to look as despicable on the outside as I felt on the inside. At first, I contended with this in secret, hidden in the refuge of my bedroom. But the cutting didn't relieve the immense strain of all that pent-up emotion.

Unable to endure the feelings any longer, I felt that the only way out was suicide. I attempted to end my life.

It was my fourth attempt in as many years and was somewhat more serious than the previous ones. Although I loved Barbara deeply, I despised myself even more and could not believe that I was worthy of love. Through my own actions, I lost my home and was placed in a children's home. Barbara wasn't to blame. Quite simply, it had become impossible to keep me safe and the help I needed was far too specialised. We still keep in contact and I will always think of Barbara as 'Mum'.

I have many memories of the time I spent in the children's home, but perhaps the most pressing and vivid of those is the death of my foster sister, Hayley. She was a pretty 16-year-old with natural white-blonde hair, blue-green eyes and a slim figure. Despite her many troubles, she was a vibrant, spirited person, usually tarrying away from the home with other streetwise young people. Hails and I led our own lives, which ran down very different tracks, but we shared many special moments that enabled us to appreciate one another's difficulties and served to create a friendship upon which we both knew we could depend.

The last time I ever saw Hayley was just a couple of days before she was killed. I remember her words so precisely, it's as though I can really hear her voice echoing in my mind. Benevolently cupping my face in the palm of her hand, she said, 'Please don't cut your face again – you're worth more than that,' and gave me a huge hug. 'We got to stick together, see, all we've got is each other.'

But all I have left of her now is many fond memories and a fading note which reads *'Love and Friendship Always, Hails. XX'*

Hayley was knocked down and killed instantly by a car whilst hitchhiking on a dual-carriageway late at night. She was alone when she died, and this knowledge still sends an icy shiver down my spine.

After a major police inquiry, the inquest heard the pathologist's conclusion that all of Hayley's injuries could not have been caused by the car, even if she went on to the road backwards. An open verdict was recorded. I firmly believe that the responsibility for this tragic loss lies with social services. Had they not refused funding for the hospital bed Hails was offered and so badly needed to treat her alcohol addiction, she would not have been on the carriageway the night she was killed. I have since been told that people within social services lost their jobs over her death. Hayley's family buried her peacefully in a town overlooking the sea, saying that her funeral was not goodbye, merely 'God bless, sleep tight'.

Hayley's death was a raw example of how precarious life could be. With this reminder of the fragility of life, I began to strive to fulfil my ambitions by enrolling in college to study science with the hope of medical school and a career as a doctor. I moved out of care and into a flat of my own, had a close group of friends and an active social life, volunteered in a primary school, held a part-time job and moved towards my dream of travel by booking and paying for a three-week holiday in Cuba.

For the first time in my life, I found inner resolution and contentment; I was at peace with myself. It had taken a lifetime to find, yet it took just a few short minutes for it all to be stolen away. The night that turned my whole world upside-down came a few days after Christmas. I was just 17 years old.

Fear and dread rose in my heart as it pounded in my chest. The tension in the room warned me of what was to come but I was paralysed, frozen, rooted to the edge of the settee. I could feel his eyes boring into the back of my head. And then it happened. He raped me.

All I could do was struggle. 'No,' I told him, '*no.*' It was like a dream, a nightmare, except I couldn't wake to free myself from this agony. This was reality. 'No.' I sobbed for a third time, knowing with dreadful certainty how pathetic and useless these words were.

When it was over, it was as though I'd been anaesthetised. All that was left in me was to curl up into a beaten heap on the toilet floor, whimpering silently. No tears came. Anguish consumed me like nothing I could describe; the physical pain that ripped through my body was merely a faint throb in comparison.

The dawn brought little fresh hope. The strength of a friend alone gave me the courage to speak aloud of my nightmare to the police. But in my trance-like state, I barely noticed. Returning home brought no solace either. I just sat, enclosed between walls, staring through nothingness into oblivion and seeing everything; each detail grotesquely perfect in my mind. The happiness I'd found a few short days before was soon so distant, untouchable.

Time lapsed. Uncaring, I remained oblivious to all but incessant reminiscence. It was not hard to become captivated by any prospect of liberation from the feelings that crippled me. So, when offered an injection of amphetamine, I accepted – so naive.

One hit is never enough. The first leads to the second, the third becomes the fourth, beginning a lifelong dependency (however long or short that life may be).

I can only describe my experiences relating to drugs as profound. The control that a tiny package of powder has over my life is incredible. It was the desire for this powder that initiated me into prostitution a month before my 18th birthday. With each new day that dawned came the eternal problem of financing my hopeless addiction. However, money played only a small part in driving me to solicit on street corners. I hated myself, despised myself even, and felt as though sex was all I was worthy of. Deeply hidden in my subconscious, this injured 'child' was so afraid; desperate not to lose control and be violated again. For me, the method of ensuring that something could not be stolen was to take control myself and give it of my own free will before it could be forcibly obtained – better to experience painful emotions as a result of my own actions than to be disempowered by anybody else's.

It didn't take long to become reliant on the quick money that ultimately provided release through drug-induced oblivion. I became trapped in a destructive cycle that ensured a fate of selling and abusing my body on a daily basis. The ferocious yearning for drugs escalated as my tolerance spiralled out of control. With drugs came misery and shame, with crazed paranoia and insanity trailing not so very far behind.

The trauma of being raped and two subsequent

burglaries, combined with amphetamine-induced delusions, was too great a strain; I fled my once-cherished flat, terror-stricken, taking with me the few possessions I still owned. Altogether, I remained homeless for nine months, taking refuge wherever I could find it: in overcrowded B&Bs, rough hostels, friends' floors, and, if all else failed, on park benches and in sheltered doorways.

During this destitute time, I began drinking heavily and using heroin and methadone as well – a lethal combination. It did not take long to become addicted. At just 18, my future was unspeakably bleak. Nevertheless, although in an acute state of melancholy, I became aware of one absolute certainty: you can choose to die at any point, but once you are dead you cannot choose to live. The survivor in me was still fighting.

I was offered a bed in a specialised drugs unit to detox from alcohol and opiates and to stabilise on a prescription of dexamphetamine, the speed substitute. I accepted, although it was perhaps the hardest decision I've ever made. One of the drugs workers told me that they had never had to work with anyone who used such a high level of amphetamine, nor anyone who was potentially as self-destructive as me.

The road to recovery was long and hard, and still is, but being in a safe environment with medication to control my flashbacks, I became more and more determined to survive. I was eventually discharged clean of all drugs and alcohol except for my daily prescription.

I once heard an old proverb that says, 'Life is what you choose to make it'. There was a time when I believed this, but not now. We are all born into a world manipulated by our predecessors, limited by class and culture, governed by authority, but mainly dominated by one thing: the search for personal gain. Circumstances beyond our control are continually moulding our lives. However, to resign yourself to these predicaments is to admit defeat. It is possible to conquer life's tribulations and I feel I am living proof of this.

I don't know what the future holds for me, but one thing I'm sure of is that at least now I *have* a future. I am waiting to go into a rehabilitation unit for a year of intensive counselling. But for now I am content just to be rebuilding my life in a positive way. And I have a sense that the many mountains I have climbed have left me ready to conquer the world.

On the Move

Kay, 19

When people say to me 'You're homeless', I reply 'No I'm not – I've got a really nice home and I'm proud of it.' Home for me is an old lorry my boyfriend and I bought from a man we met when we were living in a bender, which is a kind of home-made tent. We'd made the bender out of lots of wooden palettes and hazelwood or birch poles. It had a tarpaulin roof and a wood-burner in the middle to keep us warm, but it was leaky and we woke up one night with a stream running under us and everything covered in water. My boyfriend became ill and we needed somewhere better to stay.

The man who had the lorry before us hadn't looked after it at all. It's an old 7.5 ton British Rail truck, the next size down from a removal van. My boyfriend never trained as a carpenter but he's picked it up quickly and has made the inside of the lorry really comfortable. Our mate got us lots of tongue-and-groove wood for the walls at trade price and we found pine floorboards in a closed down hospital. There are cupboards, a bookshelf where I put all my comics, and a wardrobe, as well as a really good wood-burner. We have an L-shaped seat and a table in one corner, a cooker, and an old sink that we plumbed in ourselves and put a waterbutt underneath, with a tiled surface at the side. There's even a cage for my pet rat and space for our two dogs.

The only things I miss now are a washing machine and a bath. The site we're on is right near a laundrette, so I can do my washing there, and the other week, a friend found me a bath on a building site! I think they had been using it to mix concrete in, but we cleaned it up and last night I was able to have a bath in the lorry; it was lovely, sitting right by the wood-burner.

When we bought the lorry we got a manual straight away and we pick up the maintenance side as we go along. We need to: on one of our first journeys, the lorry overheated four times. Most people are prepared to give you help and advice, and when a bunch of lads are hanging around doing repairs, I try to look at what they are doing so that I can pick up some tips. I really want to go on an NVQ welding course so I can fix our lorry myself and make a living out of repairing others. I definitely want some sort of a job – cleaning or anything like that – but it's easier for men to pick up casual jobs, like labouring on building sites, than for girls. At the moment I'm just claiming benefits.

I couldn't live in a town or a city now, I don't like the atmosphere. It's more down to earth when you live on a site. I could never live in a council estate; it's too grim.

My boyfriend and I lived in a squat in London for a while, so we know what it's like. There was a big heroin problem there and things got really bad. I hate that scene. I've lost friends to it and one of my brothers died from it. When we moved out of London to a small community in the country, we noticed that there were fewer drugs straight away. It was a really nice site in a field next to a river. There were just seven or eight of us and it was about a mile outside the nearest town. Living on a site out of town means you have to be more organised. For example, you have to find wood for the burner, otherwise you will be cold. I suppose you have to try and grow up a bit really; you have things to do so you don't sit around drinking and getting bored.

From there we moved to a huge site that had been up and running for 12 years and had become dirty and stagnant. There were at least 100 people there at one time and the heroin problem was bad. I didn't like walking down the main drag because there were needles lying everywhere. I have a lot of friends with habits and some are OK – they don't steal everything that isn't nailed down – and I do think they deserve to have somewhere to live, too. But when you get the dealers coming on to site, things get horrible.

When we moved on, we went to another big site. There are some advantages to the bigger places, because it normally takes longer for the council to evict you. That means you have time to stay around for a while, get a job, get some money in your pocket. We moved on again a couple of months ago because we knew we were going to get evicted. Some people were saying, 'We're going to fight to keep this land', but the place had become a mud bowl. Now we're somewhere much smaller and nicer.

When you get evicted, you can get angry about why it's being done – the attitude people have towards travellers – but I think if more and more evictions happen then people will start buying yards and allowing other people to stay on them to get round the law. It's not necessarily something I want to do, but I think it's a good idea.

A few people on sites carry mobile phones or pagers so they can stay in touch with the outside world. I used to say I wouldn't have one but there have been a couple of family emergencies when it has taken a while for the message to reach me, so my mum said she would go halves with me on a pager.

Mum has always encouraged me to do what I want. I went to a convent school in North London and I wore Doc Martins and had a shaved head, so the nuns weren't too keen on me. When I was 15, I started lazing about and not going to school, and Mum said to me, 'I can shout and scream and force you to go but what's the point in that? I don't want to fall out with you.' And even when I was being a stroppy teenager she said, 'My door's always open.'

She lives in North London in a house now, but when I was young we used to have a bus and travelled round all the festivals, starting with the small ones and moving on to the bigger ones, such as Glastonbury. I suppose travelling is in my blood. I remember we had such freedom at the festivals; we were able to run about everywhere and there was such a nice atmosphere that you always felt safe.

I think there are always going to be people who travel. One family I know has three generations travelling together; a mother, father and three children and their eldest daughter has just had her second baby. I will probably want children when I'm older and I know that I will never want to bring them up in a city or on a council estate. At least on a site, I won't have to worry about them. I will try to let them have as settled a life as possible, and I will send them to school but, once they are older, you can't force them, especially if they are anything like me!

When you're a traveller, people look at you in a certain way or give you abuse just because you're leading a different life to them. But I don't care. I just think, 'Go back to your council flat and your four walls. Sit and watch your telly and be boring for the rest of your life.' I can't be bothered with people like that. I love the fresh air and the travelling; it's so nice waking up and wandering around a new town you've never been to before, and knowing that you're going to see lots of different places. I can't handle cities anymore; I suppose I must be a bit of a country bumpkin!

Making a Break

Roseanne, 18

It is impossible to say what leaving home means for everyone as each person's experiences are so different. For me, personally, it meant independence, self-worth and a sense of achievement. It's been two years since I left home and only now have I reached the point where I feel comfortable with my life. I went through a lot of emotional stress to get where I am today and I would never tell anyone that leaving home is necessarily the easiest option.

I was thrown out when I was 16 years of age because I wasn't getting on with my mum. I moved into my boyfriend's house for one week until I received a place in a women's hostel. I had my own room with a lock but the toilets, bathrooms, kitchen and lounge area were all communal. The hostel rules limited my freedom. I had to be in by 11 p.m. and I was only allowed out overnight three nights a week.

It was all so unfamiliar to me and I felt very lonely. I wasn't allowed to have guests up to see me and so I would go out and see my boyfriend every night and stay at his house every weekend. I felt he was my only escape.

The hostel depressed me so much that my college work began to suffer. I couldn't motivate myself to get out of bed in the mornings and when I did go in I couldn't be bothered to concentrate. After a month I had my first 'keywork' meeting at the hostel. This is where you can discuss whatever you like with a member of staff. After this I started to relax. I hadn't gone into the lounge/kitchen area for the first three weeks as I had felt too frightened, but after the meeting I went to watch TV and, once I had started mixing with others, life didn't seem so unbearable.

Despite this, I still spent all my free time with my boyfriend and I didn't realise how highly dependent on him I had become. Due to the fact that I lived alone, I was given an allowance of £38.90 per week. £7 of that went towards a service charge at the hostel and £20 went towards shopping for food and essentials. After expenses I was left with about £10 a week, but that didn't matter because my boyfriend always used to take me out. I hardly ever saw my other friends at this time except at school because I couldn't afford to go out with them.

After eight months I was used to life in the hostel. I didn't enjoy it, but I accepted it. At this point I heard that I would be moving to a foyer and it seemed much more promising.

In the foyer I stayed in a flat with two bedrooms so I only had to share a bathroom and kitchen with one other person. There was no curfew, I was allowed guests in my room and after three months. I was allowed to have overnight guests three times a week. My quality of life began to improve; I made new friends with the people who live here and old friendships became strong again.

Everything was perfect for the first three months at the foyer. But then my neighbour, who was only 24, died in a motorcycle accident, and it shook me a lot. It was the first heavy emotion I'd experienced since leaving home. The night he died I called my boyfriend's house at 6 a.m. and he came over. I really needed him at this time, more than ever, so when he told me that he had to go to work it hurt me a lot.

Because he wasn't there for me when I needed support, I drew my strength from spending time with the brother of my late friend. For three weeks I left my boyfriend in the cold and clung to the brother, as if it prevented me from having to say goodbye to my friend. The inevitable happened and I ended up having sex with this guy, which simply made matters worse. After the sex I wanted to be held by him every night. I had been strong before and now I wanted someone to be strong for me. When he wasn't, I found I couldn't eat or sleep. I totally lost my grip on reality, and it was only at the funeral three weeks later, when I finally did say goodbye to my neighbour, that I started to get better.

Once things began to slip back to normal I found that I resented my boyfriend for having let me down at a time when I needed him. I felt that the whole scenario was his fault but I pushed it to the back of my mind and just tried to get along with things. I had been with him for such a long time that I couldn't bear the thought of losing him.

The problem obviously didn't go away and we kept having major arguments. Every time we had a really big bust-up, I found that I couldn't cope with the tension it produced, so I turned to self-harm. If I could just draw blood from myself the stress was relieved.

Things continued like this for months. My boyfriend was very worried about me and wanted me to get help. I thought that I didn't need it but pretended that I would see someone just to keep the peace.

I knew that what I was doing was wrong but I also knew I didn't need help; my self-harm addiction was caused by one particular thing, and that thing was my boyfriend.

Eventually I found the strength to split with him. It was one of the hardest things I've ever had to do, but the split made me realise how dependent I was on him. My self-harm problem was a result of my fear of losing both him and the stability that the relationship offered. Because my life was so unstable in other areas I hooked on to my relationship, which turned out to be a very dangerous situation to be in.

It was very hard not to go back to him. The split meant that I lost his financial support and suddenly I had a lot more time on my hands. After living in someone's pocket for two years it was a very lonely experience. I was unemployed and not in college at that point, so I generally sat indoors all day everyday wasting any money I had on drinking with my friends.

After a while, however, the pain started to fade and I felt able to take control of my life (and my finances) again. I realised that I didn't have to be surrounded by people all of the time and being alone made me appreciate the time with my friends instead of taking them for granted.

I was also determined to get a job and even though I did not get my first choice, I have just completed a training course and will be moving out of London to start a new job, and a new life, soon.

Maturing allows you to see things clearly and realise your true aims. It was only the split with my boyfriend that brought me the independence that I treasure so much today. It was a very difficult stage to reach but one that makes you realise that you are worth something. Now that I've had my independence, I would never let anyone take it away.

A Second Chance

Danielle, 19

I first became homeless in Belfast when I was 14. My mum and dad had split up when I was young and I'd been moved around different relatives in Northern Ireland. I was always drinking and staying out all night, so I used to get asked to move on a lot by people, including my dad, who was living with a girlfriend at the time and who told me to go and not bother him again.

The first time I came to London was with a boyfriend who was 20. He was a punk and he knew some other punks living in Camden. We saw a guy at the station who looked like a punk and he took us back to his squat. It smelled bad but we had nowhere else to go. We had to sleep in the living-room, and one night when we were drunk we set the *Yellow Pages* on fire. The next thing I remember is being dragged out by firemen. It wasn't a nice experience.

There were no mirrors in the squat and I didn't know how dirty I was until I went to use the toilet in a burger bar. I was nasty looking, with big spots all over my cheeks and funny-looking eyes. It got too much; it was freezing and depressing so I went back to Belfast. My boyfriend stayed on.

When I got back the social workers were going to put me into care; they said I had behavioural problems because of my drinking. They wanted to put me in this training school for girls, which is like a young offenders' institute, but my granny said no way was I going in there, so she let me stay with her. You could get put in that school for a number of reasons, such as your own safety if you were being abused, but you'd be mixing with others who were there for doing things such as joyriding and shoplifting. I know one girl who was there for her own safety. She'd done nothing wrong, but she ended up riding in stolen cars. Her head's really been done in by that place.

On my 16th birthday I went with another boyfriend to Dublin and we stayed in a bedsit with his friend. It was tiny. His friend slept in a single bed and we slept on the floor. There was no privacy. The friend was a junkie and we ended up doing lots of drugs. I got into drugs because I felt my life was out of control, and so I began to behave in a way that was out of control too. I just wanted the whole world to be blurred so that I didn't have to think about anything.

By this time I hadn't spoken to my dad for two years. I thought I hated him because of the way he'd thrown me out. On St Patrick's night my boyfriend and I had got

27

really drunk and we had a fight. He smashed my face against a metal bridge. I was crying and crying, and I phoned my dad and asked him to come and get me. When he turned up he was shocked at how I looked: my face was all bruised. Dad phoned a women's refuge to see if they'd take me but they said I was too young. I decided to stay in Dublin and give it another go and my dad headed off back home.

I was doing a lot of drugs and by this time I was even injecting into my hands. They'd become all swollen and infected so I had to go to hospital to get them treated. I was sitting there in the hospital looking at my hands, with a boyfriend who beat the shit out of me, thinking, What am I doing? I'm only 16. So I called my dad again and this time I went back with him to Belfast.

The thing is, nobody really helped me sort out what was going on in my head, so it wasn't long before I went back to my old ways: running about, drinking, clubbing and shoplifting. I kept getting caught by the police. Once they even thought of keeping me on remand in a cell over Christmas, which really scared me.

When I was 17 I was sent to court for shoplifting and something happened that I think was a turning point for me. Quite simply, the judge was nice to me. He asked me what I wanted to do with my life. I told him I wanted to be a youth worker. He started having a conversation with me in front of everyone in the court, as I was standing there in the dock. He could have sent me to prison but instead he gave me a fine. But he also said it was my last chance. He was so lovely. I couldn't believe he was interested in me and wanted to have a conversation with me. Normally you expect judges to be old with grey hair and glasses perched on their noses. This one saw me as a person instead of a troublemaker. He helped me and made me feel positive, as if I really could make something of my life. This was the first time anyone had treated me with a bit of understanding.

I wrote the judge a letter but didn't post it. I wanted to thank him and to say maybe this was just a day's work for him, but it had really changed things for me.

After that I went on a youth-training programme and things calmed down. I was still going to the pub but just having one drink and then going home. I was mixing with people on the programme and I'm still friendly with most of them. I did retailing, computers, hair-dressing and office work. Then I found out I'd got a flat. I'd put myself on the council list when I was 16, so it had taken two years. The flat was unfurnished and I had no money, but I got the priest in to bless it, anyway. It was my home and I had so many hopes for it.

I saved and got some nice wallpaper and a carpet, but then things started to go wrong. The flat was broken into, the door smashed in and the locks broken off. I had a fair idea who had done it and they were people living on the same estate. A week later it was broken into again and this time my clothes were stolen.

The night before my 18th birthday I'd been working the late shift at a taxi office. I finished at 4 a.m. and got a cab home. From the road you could see my bedroom; there were lights on and people walking about in my flat. I asked the driver to wait and went to see who it was. I walked in and recognised the people who had broken in. When they saw me they all started running towards the door. One of them had a bag of my stuff and I made a grab for it. The man let go but punched me on his way out. I ran after them and the taxi-driver called the police. They'd stolen stupid things: my dairy, shampoo. I just thought to myself, Happy Birthday, Danielle.

I didn't even get the council to come and put the locks back on this time. I couldn't give a shit any more. I'd asked for a loan to get a metal security grill but the council said it would be a fire risk. One of my friends was going to Wales to work in a holiday camp and she asked me if I wanted to go, too. So I went, leaving the door to the flat wide open behind me.

We moved round a couple of holiday camps, went back and forth to Belfast, and came to London this summer. I hadn't had my period for a couple of months but I wasn't too bothered because it was sometimes late if I'd taken drugs or was stressed. Then I had a dream about a wee baby girl wearing pink leggings and the next morning I felt sick. I knew I had to go and find out for sure.

I went to a day centre and one of the day workers I knew did a pregnancy test. I was fairly sure it was going to be negative, so when she told me it was positive I just put my hands to my mouth and started to cry. She asked me if I wanted an abortion but I said no way. It's not because I'm a Catholic – I believe every woman has the right to choose – but for me, personally, a life is a life from the moment of conception. The worker said there were other alternatives, such as fostering or adoption, but I said no.

When I got back to the hostel I was staying in, I desperately needed someone to talk to. I wanted someone who would listen and reassure me. Instead the worker I spoke to would only say negative things. She said I would be pushing the baby out on my own, that my friends weren't going to want to know me, that I'd be better off having an abortion.

I think it's important that I go back to Belfast now. At least I know I won't starve there. I have friends and they'll help me out. I know I'll have to do most things on my own, but the environment there will be better for me and the baby. London can be a very cold place if you haven't got any money; people can be cold towards you.

A couple of weeks ago I got really bad pains and I was taken to the hospital. They thought I was having an ectopic pregnancy, which means the baby is growing outside the womb. It was the scariest experience of my life. Before this I was in shock and I kept thinking to myself, What am I doing? My life is over. All my plans are finished and I'm going to have to do everything by myself. I thought it would all be too much responsibility. But that night, when the nurse told me the baby might not survive, I couldn't stop crying and I started to pray, saying I'd give up smoking and drinking and doing drugs if this baby survived. It made me realise how much I loved this baby already. I think it's going to be a girl. I always said I wanted to be 28 or 30 before I had any kids, but sometimes things are just meant to happen.

Before I was pregnant I used to smoke a lot of crack. It's very addictive and I was getting hooked, but now that I'm pregnant I know all that's got to stop. I got pregnant when I was smoking with a friend; one thing just led to another. He's older than me and when I phoned to tell him, his immediate response was that I was trying to blackmail him. I'm not. I don't want anything from him. I just thought he had a right to know. But he doesn't seem to care much; I've called him since and he hasn't got back in touch. He was an old friend, too.

I want to try and keep in touch with him for the sake of my child. I know what it's like, growing up with insecurity, and I want my child to know who its father is. He or she will be of mixed race, which is unusual in Belfast, and I am worried about racism. I think it will be easier for the kid if it stays in touch with its dad. But, above all, I want my child to have a secure life and to know that it's loved. I want to keep it clean and healthy and never let it go hungry. I remember when I was hungry, I used to have to eat sugar sandwiches. I don't want that for my baby.

Street Love

Vanessa, 17

I've been homeless for six years now and before that I was in care. I'd been in care since the age of 11 because I kept running away from school, playing truant, getting suspended and expelled. Mum and Dad had just been through a divorce and I think that had a lot to do with it.

I couldn't handle being in care; I was very independent and I guess I just liked doing my own thing. I was always being moved from home to home and I couldn't settle anywhere. Either I didn't like it, or I'd upset the staff, or it was too far from anyone I knew. I wanted to be close to my mum and dad in London even though I wasn't in contact with them anymore.

I did try foster care and that didn't work either. I was put with a lady who was supposed to be suitable and it turned out she was on every tranquilliser and sleeping pill going. Then I went to another home that already had six or seven foster children and it was brilliant for the first couple of months. But, after a while, it was all too much for me. There was so much going on with the other children. They were very much a family and I was very much an outsider.

When I left there I got moved around different places until finally I went to work in Wales with a lady on a farm. I stayed there a long time and I became part of the family, but the lady started presuming I would work all the time. I loved what I was doing, but I needed a break and I never got one. Seven days a week I worked, and I began to feel I was missing out. I ended up having a really big argument and walking out. I just upped and left. I guess that's when I truly became homeless.

People seem to think you put yourself on the streets, but that's not true; the care system does a good job of it themselves.

I was begging the other day and this girl of about 13 came up to me and started asking me dodgy questions: how much money I made, where I was sleeping and so on. She obviously had some sort of learning difficulty, so me and my friend took her to a police station. It turned out she was in care (her carers were at the station waiting for her), and all she would say was that she didn't like it. Whenever you go into a children's home you always get two groups of people: one lot who all get on well and think it's OK, and the other lot who don't say a word.

There are always going to be outsiders with the system the way it is. It needs to be completely revised. At the moment it just assumes that by the time you're 16, you can cope on your own and quite often you can't. You are supposed to go from a big children's home, where there is always something going on, to a tiny bedsit where you have to do everything yourself. A lot of people just can't hack it.

When I left care, I stayed with friends at first. I didn't want to be in the same place all the time so I'd hitch to another, making friends along the way and staying where I could.

The worst place I stayed was sleeping on the streets of Bristol. There were a lot of drunks and heroin addicts, people trying to nick whatever money you had, and you could never get a decent night's sleep. I used to find somewhere where other people were sleeping – in a well-lit high street – or where there were cameras. It's true what they say about there being safety in numbers. I slept rough in the Bullring in Waterloo for a while and that was OK because you always meet new people and they accept you for who you are; they don't judge you the way 'normal' people would.

If you're homeless and meet other homeless people at least you're all in the same boat. Normal housed society looks at you and only sees the scruffy side. I was begging one night about four or five days ago and a woman, her husband and three children were walking past. She stopped to give me some money and her husband turned round and said, right in front of me, 'No, don't give her any money. She'll only spend it on drugs.' I told him that if I wanted to spend it on drugs I would, but I was actually trying to get money for food. People just want to stereotype you. If you're on the street you're either a beggar, a thief, a drug addict or a drunk. You're always something; something bad.

I've had untold amounts of fights. When you're begging people tend to get a bit shitty with you. You'll always get someone coming up to you and saying, 'Get a job, get a life'. As if it's that simple.

When you're begging at night things do get a bit leery because there are usually a lot more drunks about. Believe it or not, they tend to give more trouble to the men than the women. I was with a guy a couple of weeks ago and we asked a group of men if they could spare us any change. One turned round, came back, and tried to stab my friend in the back of the head with a Coke can. Luckily his friends stopped him, saying, 'Leave them alone, they're only trying to make a living'. They gave us a tenner, but it doesn't make up for them being rude in the first place.

The thing is, you tend to get used to it. At the end of the day people can think you're scum, say 'Get a life' or whatever, but you need enough money to live and buy clothes, food, and do the things 'normal' people do. I just wish 'normal' society would remember that.

One thing society forgets is that homeless people have relationships just like everyone else. I met my fiancee about one and a half years ago in Dorset. We just got talking one day. I'd got quite heavily into the drugs scene and was using amphetamines, and he was on heroin. Like many homeless people we'd got into drugs through sheer boredom and lack of self-confidence, but it's also because drugs are always in your face. We both wanted to come off drugs so we decided to do it together.

It's very hard – very few people understand quite how hard – to come off drugs. For people who live in a house and have friends and family, it's easier. You can stay in all day, take the methadone the doctor's given you and basically get through it. I'm not saying it's not hard, it is. But when you're on the streets it's a lot, lot tougher. You've got drugs in your face 24 hours a day, seven days a week and there's nowhere you can just take yourself off to avoid it.

We managed to last a long time before we touched drugs again. Then one day I was with a friend and lo and behold he had a bag of heroin. He asked me if I'd like to try some. I did, and I liked it. A few days later I was with my fiance and we met this bloke who was selling heroin. My fiance said he'd like some because he'd been off it for so long and wanted a treat. It doesn't take much to get a habit, it's so addictive. You only need to try it once or twice and it hits you. That's why so many people have a problem. Soon I was on a £70- to £80-a-day habit, and he was on £100 a day. We were shoplifting, busking, begging, all kinds of things.

But we were lucky. We managed to find a really good GP who gave us stuff that stops you withdrawing when you come off the drugs, and we found a temporary night shelter so we had somewhere to stay. It takes about three to four weeks to make you feel normal again.

My fiance and I got engaged in September. We were due to get married in January but we didn't have any money so we'll probably leave it until we're settled. At the moment we sleep in car parks because it's safer than sleeping in shop doorways. Even in a car park, where it's quite sheltered and warm, you always have to sleep with one eye open and all your stuff close by. That's why so many homeless people have dogs. They're not just good companions, they're also very protective and loyal to you. We're going to get one soon. A lot of people imagine that street dogs are neglected but they probably get fed more than normal house dogs!

I rely on my fiance a hell of a lot; he's always there for me. If I'm begging he stays somewhere he can see me in case I get into trouble and I always have him near to me at night when I go to sleep. There's no side to him and he's said to me that we've been together so long now we just seem to be a part of each other. If we're not together, it always feels like there's something missing and we walk around completely lost. We both need each other. It goes a lot further than just being lovers; he's my best friend, he's my family, he's everything I need in one person. I know he'll never leave me and I'll never leave him, so he's something continuous in a life with so little continuity. Everything else changes, you're always having to move on.

We want to find somewhere to live now. We've talked about settling down and getting a house and basically it seems like the right thing to do. We both love travelling but we can still use a house as a base and go away for weekends knowing we've got somewhere to come back to. Because we're not socially acceptable, people don't realise we do what normal people do. Just like everyone else, we want to love each other and be together.

Carry on Squatting!

Linnea, 18

I was born in December 1979 in the north of Sweden, where the mountains are snowy and the winters long and cold. My mum and dad are two old hippies, and I suppose that with me came the very end of their 'wild days'.

We lived in a big wooden house in the middle of a forest. Early in my life, we all moved down to the middle of Sweden, where I went to school, and spent most of my childhood and early teenage years. We lived outside a small town called Arvika, in an idyllic neighbourhood – again right inside the forest. I think this calm forest environment helped me a lot in later life; it made me a peaceful person.

I went to school in the forest with about 40 other children and, until the age of 12, I was completely unaware of the outside world, isolated and quite happy in this little world of my own.

Then I changed schools. It was in town and was horrible and dirty. My burning passion for music helped me survive those unhappy years. I played many instruments, mostly bass guitar and cello, and I loved singing. I actually started in a music school, but after half a year I gave it up. My classmates were so different from me, and I wasn't enjoying it.

After that I went to an art school for one and a half years. I had so many interests that I didn't know what to do! I'm glad that my parents let me try different things; they were wonderful.

When I was about 15 a weird period in my life began. Looking back, I don't know why I behaved the way I did, but I started to hang around with horrible friends who didn't have a good effect on me. I drank a lot, and I bunked off school. All my passion for life, my love of art and music, seemed to disappear for a while. I used to drink so much that I had no idea what I'd been doing – everything was a complete blank. I didn't seem to care about anything, even myself. My life felt like a stairway leading downwards.

But luckily this came to an end. By the summer of 1996, when I was 16, I started to do more things that had a positive effect on me, such as meditation, yoga and dance. I started to think seriously about what I wanted to do with my life. I felt quite different from my friends and realised that one of the reasons I had been so destructive was the peer pressure. I wanted to get away from this small, narrow-minded town, where no one seemed to care about more spiritual things. I had so many dreams about how I wanted to live. I wanted freedom. Desperately.

So my friend and I decided to do something drastic.

Her older sister was studying in Brighton at the time, and really liked it. Four months later, me and my friend were both sitting on an aeroplane, on our way to England.

Brighton. I really felt that my life was going to change. My friend had a job in a family as an au pair, and I stayed with her for three weeks. Then I found a family myself and moved in. I had to look after their three-year-old daughter and she was wonderful, but it was like slave labour. I did all the housework, cleaning, washing, washing up, ironing, and cooking, plus full-time child care. I only had a few nights and Sundays free each week.

In my spare time I explored this exciting new place. Of course, I was terribly homesick in the beginning but, after a few weeks, I was fine. I really like Brighton; it has such a good feeling about it. A whole new world opened up in front of my eyes, a whole new culture. I began to feel at home very quickly.

I had to communicate in this new language, which of course I'd been learning at school, but I still felt totally uncomfortable with it. It took a while but now it almost feels like my main language.

In October something important happened; I met the man of my dreams. It was totally unexpected. He just turned up one rainy Wednesday in a nightclub, a 17-year old called Luke. Everything was perfect from the start, we got on so well. The next night he took me to a really nice 'alternative' cafe and since then, it's been him and no one else.

Just before Christmas I moved in with him. He lived in an extremely small bedsit that he had just managed to get after being homeless for years. I really liked the place at first, but after a while it put a strain on both of us because it was so small, had no heating and the roof leaked. But it was ours, the first place of our own, and that made it very special.

The trouble was money. I don't get any benefits, as I'm not English, so we had to share Luke's dole money and it wasn't enough to cover the electricity or the rent. So we decided to move into the squat we are in at the moment. I don't mind squatting; it's a good solution to homelessness. The only bad thing about it is that you can get into trouble with landlords and bailiffs, and that sort of thing. You can't really relax when you know you might have to move out quickly.

Luke's dole money is quite a small amount, but we seem to manage OK. It can be quite scary to be relying on somebody else, but maybe one day it will be the other way around. We share the squat with some other young people and buy food together, which seems to make it less expensive. I like living in a sort of commune with lots of people; everything is much more fun!

I still keep in touch with my mum and dad. They don't really accept my lifestyle, but I suppose they just care about me and don't understand why I won't move back to Sweden, or why I don't want to go to school or get a job. They really love me, and I love them, but I wish that they could understand me more, see what's inside. I suppose all parents worry about the future but, the thing is, I don't even know what I'm doing tomorrow, let alone in five years time!

What I am trying to say is that I have changed, and I don't want to change back. Going to school now would be like going backwards. I would like to attend an art course, because I love painting and photography. At the moment I can't really afford any proper materials, so I paint on whatever comes my way: walls, boots, odd pieces of paper. I also like writing and find poetry very inspiring.

I don't want to get a normal job, because I hate the whole way capitalist society works. My dream would be to live in a cottage in the countryside with Luke and grow my own vegetables. I would like to have children, and it would be a good place for them to grow up.

Me and Luke are going to have a pagan wedding on the beach this year. I really love him and want to stay with him forever. I have changed so much since I met him, and he has taught me so many things.

I love this alternative lifestyle, where you're free to do what you want with your life. The people I know here seem to be so much more mature and generous than the people I used to know in Sweden. I also think it is more usual in a middle-class society to be greedy and narrow-minded, and not to accept those who are different from you. When you have got a lot of things, you just want more. When you haven't got much, you're quite happy with what you have. I know you can't generalise, but the people living here in squats seem to be much more able to share. Some people might wonder how you can choose a poor lifestyle, when you had 'everything' before. It might sound like a cliché but, in the end, freedom and love are the only things that matter.

What I miss about the life I used to have in Sweden is my home, getting food on a plate every day, and being able to be a 'child'; but I've left that behind now. At first I was a bit confused and wondered 'am I doing the right thing?' But I know I'll be OK. My life is full of things that I love, spending time with brilliant, real friends, and doing meaningful things, such as being involved in animal rights. I never, ever want to be part of the 'normal' world again. I just can't!

All that Glitters . . .

Isha, 19

Last week my ex-boyfriend was hanging around the hostel where I live and when I went outside to go to the garage, he attacked me. He kept saying he only wanted to talk, but he started to drag me along the road. My slippers fell off and I grabbed hold of a fence to stop myself being pulled along. But the metal caught my side and I got hurt.

We'd been going out since I was 16, and we broke up in January of this year. It's been very difficult for me because he found out where I moved to and he stalks me and harasses me. He's been violent; he's even phoned up and threatened to kill me. I've told the police but they haven't helped. They seemed to listen at first and said they could come with me to his workplace to give him a warning, but when I called to see how they were getting on with my case, they told me they couldn't find any records of my reports against him; so, as far as they were concerned, nothing had happened. I have tried to take an injunction out against him but the police say I need a minimum of ten reports. They did put me in touch with the domestic-violence unit last year. I couldn't get hold of them for ages and, when I did, all I was offered was counselling. The unit was supportive in one sense, but I needed something legal.

My boyfriend was never a violent partner when I was going out with him – he never hit me – but he did have a drink problem and that's why I didn't want to be with him anymore. It made his moods so changeable I couldn't handle it. I did still love him and tried to help him. He doesn't have anyone; he's an only child, his mother lives in America and he doesn't speak to her because his stepfather used to beat him up all the time. The stepfather used to beat my boyfriend's mother, too, and my boyfriend could never forgive her for not leaving him. But now my ex hangs on to 'us' when there *is* no 'us' anymore; I keep telling him that. As far as he is concerned I'm 'his', and he keeps coming out with this 'If I can't have you, no one will' kind of attitude.

I left home partly because of him. He was phoning me all hours of the night and I felt that he was becoming a burden to my mother as well as to me. But mainly I decided to leave because I suffered domestic violence from my younger brother, who is 16 but much bigger than me. He was verbally abusive, calling me everything under the sun, and my mum didn't allow me to discipline him.

My brother is disturbed; he's got some kind of problem. He has been through a lot of things, he's seen too much, and I think it has affected the way he lives. He is very violent and has hit my mum on one occasion. He even got expelled from primary school – I mean, who gets kicked out of primary school?

Anyway, things came to a head one night when he started threatening me with a knife. It was two in the morning and my mum wanted me to leave the house and go and stay with one of her friends. I hadn't done anything wrong and yet she was telling me to go. She couldn't deal with the situation and called the police. Instead of talking to my brother, the police escorted *me* out, so I went to a friend's house. We're both Eritrean, from Ethiopia, although I have lived in London for most of my life. I stayed with her for the weekend and then went to the council homeless unit, who put me in a hostel in South London. That was about a year ago. There were no staff at this place, apart from a cleaner who came for two hours Monday to Friday. There was no support, no resettlement officer; there was nothing.

I had been there for about four months when I heard that my cousin, who has diabetes, had been rushed into hospital in Birmingham. I headed straight there and stayed for about seven days but, when I returned, I found that all the locks to my room had been changed and someone else was living there. All my things had been packed up and put into storage. It was 1 a.m., it was St Valentine's Day, and I was homeless again.

Apparently I should have notified the social workers before I went away. I did notify the landlady of the hostel, but it didn't count unless I notified my caseworker, too. I had tried, but I hadn't been able to get hold of her. I had to stay with friends over the weekend and went back to the council homeless unit first thing on Monday morning.

There I was told it wasn't the council's duty to rehouse

me as I had failed to fulfil my tenancy agreement. They said I had to find somewhere to live myself, then notify my caseworker of my whereabouts. But I wasn't going to take this lying down. I sat there all day, from 10 a.m. until closing time, and insisted on seeing the manager. She allocated me a housing officer and eventually I was transferred to the hostel I am in now, although they did make it very clear that this placement was independent of the council. My persistence had paid off!

When I first came here I liked it. It's very clean and the staff are friendly. I wasn't too keen on the idea of sharing a room with two others because I was scared they might go through my stuff and steal things, but I needn't have worried; my room-mates are really nice. Still, it didn't stop me from feeling lonely and scared. It wasn't really to do with being by myself but more to do with feeling unprotected and insecure about my future. I didn't know anyone here well enough to confide in them, and I didn't know where I would be staying next. I was told I'd be rehoused again in six months, but where?

At least it was a step forward. I knew I couldn't go back to living at home again. Mum wanted me to come back after the night my brother threatened me but, as far as I was concerned, she'd made a decision when she asked me to leave. I did understand how difficult things were for her, though. My brother was so out of control Mum was afraid of him. My older brother, who had been like the father figure of our family, had left home and felt that our younger brother wasn't his problem anymore. He had sorted himself out, got a home of his own, and a job as a graphic designer.

I don't think the place where we lived when we were younger helped much, either. It was a very bad council estate. Mum was desperate for the council to move us out but we were there for ten years. My sister got mugged; I was jumped and then threatened with a barbecue fork; a lot of the boys on the estate started using and selling crack; and we had our house burgled five times by addicts. We even had a gun pulled on us on our own doorstep and still the council wouldn't move us. Mum was suicidal and cried every night.

Thankfully Mum got moved recently. Things haven't been easy for her. There are five of us and she managed to raise us all on her own. I haven't seen my father since I was five so I think they're separated, but I'm not sure. We were told that our father would be coming over to England after us and all these years I've been waiting, not really knowing.

But we were always well fed and well looked after. Mum dressed us in nice clothes and we never went to school looking like tramps. My brother got picked on because his clothes looked so good and I think that the bullying affected him a lot. It was a boys school and I think that made the bullying worse. Other kids were always trying to steal his sneakers or his jacket.

I am looking forward now in the sense that I've applied to two colleges. I'm waiting to hear from one and I can enrol in the other next week. I've got an interview for a flat and I'm really excited about it because this place can be very stressful and depressing. A lot of people staying here don't tend to have a life outside it but some, like me, have work as well. At the moment I do agency work as a silver-service waitress, because my benefits allow me to earn a small amount of money. But it's not frequent, and it's out of the blue when it happens. I can't rely on it.

I am used to working. I've done waitressing and reception work, and did work experience at a law firm. The firm actually offered me a position but my mum wanted me to go to college to do my A levels. I started studying for them but my boyfriend used to wait for me outside the college or enter the premises, looking for me, so I stopped going. One day he literally took my school books and my bag off me and wouldn't give them back.

I haven't led him on. Every time I hear his voice on the phone I hang up and if I see him walking down the street I head in the opposite direction. But he seems to have no understanding of the situation at all, he really doesn't. He's made threats to my family – my mum, in particular. He's let down one of her tyres and kicked down her door. She has high blood pressure and is on medication, so I worry about her. She's getting old before her time. If I do get a place now and he finds out where it is, it will be living hell. But I can't live my life looking over my shoulder the whole time.

I suppose moving out was a good thing in some ways. It meant that at least my ex wasn't going round my mum's looking for me the whole time. I do see her a lot now and I've forgiven her. At the end of the day she's my mother, the one who pushed me out into the world, and I reckon she's at the age where her children should start looking after her, not the other way round.

So, I'm trying to get myself back on my feet and live a normal, decent life without anyone troubling me – no men, no relationships, nothing. I get on well with men as friends and it's nice to go out for a meal or to the movies with no strings attached. But some want a relationship and I'm just not ready for that. How can I get into a relationship when I'm homeless, I haven't got a base and have no money in the bank? I need to get myself together before I invest in anything else.

Words of wisdom as a final thought. A very wise person with a beautiful heart once told me all that glitters is not gold. That has certainly been my experience and I have learnt to be careful about who I trust. But also, as my mother always said, give respect where respect is due, and that includes self-respect; ensure that you love yourself to the full. I'm looking ahead now and am determined to live life as a leader, not a follower.

No Excuse

Stephanie, 16

My dad has been hitting me for eight years of my life – since I was seven years old. I don't know why he's always picked on me rather than my mum or my brother. I've been told it's because he has a stressful job, but I don't think that's any sort of excuse at all.

I think it could be because he isn't my real father. My mum was married before and was having an affair with my present dad when her first husband died. I was born about six months later. Mum and Dad married before I was born. I first questioned whether he was my real dad when he started hitting me and it has always been in the back of my mind. I decided I really wanted to know the truth, but when I asked him, he refused to have a DNA test.

I feel I can get on better with my family if I'm not actually living with them. I miss my mum, my brother, the cat and the fish. We have a huge house, a big garden, two cars in the drive, but I'd rather be on the streets than living, at home. That says a lot.

This year, I just had enough; I couldn't cope with the violence any more. So I went into town, met up with some mates, and they agreed to help me get into a squat the next day.

I left for school as usual and waited at the end of the road until my dad's car had gone. Then I went back and picked up my stuff.

The squat was in the centre of town. I stayed a couple of nights and left my bags there but most of the stuff got nicked. I also had all my hair cut off so it would be harder to track me down. Then I moved to a hostel for 16-25-year olds for one night. I had to lie about my age because I wasn't quite 16. I preferred staying at the squat to the hostel because I had to sleep in a dormitory with girls slagging each other off all the time.

A friend was hitching to another town and I decided to join him so I could keep on the run. We slept outside in doorways, then inside a big shed, before we got thrown out by monks who owned the land it was on. (Goodness knows what chucking us out did for their karma; aren't they supposed to be nice to people with no money?) From there we stayed in a hut where the roof caved in and soaked us. By this time all I had left was a vanity case with clean knickers in it.

Then one night I decided to ring Mum. But my parents dialled 1471 and found out where I was. I'd already heard the police were on to me. They'd found my hair in the squat and had produced a photo of me without any hair to show round my home town. My parents came down to the town I was in, but couldn't find me. Then, one morning, I'd just sat down to eat some porridge in a day centre, when one of the workers told me the police were waiting for me outside. They weren't allowed to come in, but I thought I might as well get it over with, so I went with them to the local police station.

I was there until 4 p.m. when my parents showed up. Eventually I was told by someone from social services that they couldn't help me and I'd have to go to my own home town to get help. My parents bundled me into my dad's car, put the child locks on, and wound up the windows. My mum was screaming and crying and my dad had this look on his face that I knew meant he was going to hit me. I was thinking, 'Oh shit – I'm going to die when I get home.' And I did get beaten up.

So, two days later I was off again and returned to the town where they'd picked me up. Of course, the police soon turned up again but this time they just rang my mum, who said I should stay in that place as long as I phoned her once a week. She wasn't happy, but she knew I would just run away again if they brought me back. So she left it at that.

After the hut, the person I was travelling with and I found another squat: a big derelict building. Three of us moved in at first, then more and more people came, until there were too many. I was seeing someone who was 30, and a heroin addict. It was his fault. We lost control of the squat when he decided to let all his smack-addict friends come and stay. I don't touch the stuff and he kept nicking all my money or 'borrowing' it and not paying it back, so I decided to break up with him.

My new boyfriend moved to this town after leaving the army. He was homeless at first, but now he has a job and a bedsit. We're going to try to get a bigger flat, and I'm going to look for a job and claim benefits. It's hard to get a job when you don't have a proper address. At the moment I only make money from begging, so my boyfriend works really hard to support us.

Before I left home I had a job lined up working as a trainee solicitor's clerk and I was going to do a part-time college course. Now I just want anything that pays well. I would like to go back to college and finish my GCSEs – I know I could get my exams because I did well at school – but if it costs money, I won't do it. When you leave home, your priorities have to change.

My boyfriend persuaded me to go home to my parents a week ago to give it another try and to make sure I didn't have any regrets about leaving. My dad was the same as usual. Mum was trying hard to make Dad stop and he started beating her and my brother, too. I never saw him doing that before, so I battered him with a chair and he kicked me out. I wasn't being a bitch – I was just defending my family – but it makes me more sure than ever that I've done the right thing.

It's a Rich Man's World

Victoria, 18

I came to England with my grandparents seven years ago. My mum lives in Barbados and she didn't get along with my grandparents at all. So, when I started having problems with them about a year and a half ago, they kept telling me I was just like her.

My older sister also moved to London with us but she left and went to live in a hostel. When I argued with my grandparents they said I was being naughty and rude, and that I was copying my sister. They said I could go and live in a hostel, too.

Then one day things got really bad. There was a huge argument, a lot of noise, and the police were called. So I left in the clothes I was wearing and went to a day centre in South London, where they found me a hostel to stay in.

I lived in the hostel for a couple of months and then moved to where I am now. It's called a 'foyer', which means you get somewhere to live and help with training and jobs at the same time. It's mixed accommodation but you can only share with a person of the same sex, so I share a flat with another girl. There are always different activities going on and they've got staff 24 hours a day. I've also got a link worker I can go to if I need to sort anything out.

At the foyer, you have to search for jobs at least three times a week, but there's a room with newspapers, a telephone, and the Internet to help you. You have to sign in to a logbook to prove you are looking. The logbooks are checked regularly and your flat is health-and-safety checked once a month.

When I came to the foyer I had to do an action plan within the first month about what sort of training or job I wanted. I really want to go into the travel industry but at the moment I am looking for work as an office junior, just to get some money. I'd like to have a steady job, a flat and a car; just to live comfortably, I suppose.

Money is the biggest problem when you haven't got a job. If you are on your own you have to sort out housing benefit and income support by yourself, but here there are staff who can help you.

My flat mate and I help each other. She's a couple of years older than me but we've got the same problems, so we understand each other and can talk about them. We know what it's like to get your giro when the money runs out the same day. You have to make sure your rent is paid and you're left with nothing for the week.

I'm in rent arrears so I have to pay £25 every two weeks instead of £7. This is because when I was working over Christmas as an office temp I had to pay full rent but

I didn't realise this, so I owe extra for that time.

I still keep in touch with Mum but I don't want to go back to Barbados. I want to live here. Perhaps I'll visit her when I get my own place but at the moment I can't really take time out from looking for a job. My sister is now 21, she's got a son, a job as a hospital cook, and a two-bedroom furnished flat. I want everything she has apart from the son. I don't want children, I just want a career.

On the whole I think I've managed better than some. If you need constant attention it's quite difficult to cope on your own. I know some of my friends who have lived in hostels just couldn't manage; they had to move on or go home.

I'm still in contact with quite a few of my school friends, because I live in the same area where I went to school, and some of the people I have met here are friends of friends.

In my spare time I go to clubs or to the cinema with any money left over from my dole cheque. I get £79 every two weeks but when you take away rent and £30 for food there isn't much left, maybe £10, so I don't go out much.

I really have to budget. That's what the foyer's taught me: being responsible. When I fell into arrears they gave me a rent agreement that I must follow until I'm paid up to date. I'd be alright if I had a job. I've had quite a few interviews and have filled out lots of application forms. I'm just waiting for responses.

When I was with my grandparents they told me what it would be like one day when I had to manage my own affairs. Now I'm doing it and I've learnt so much. The only thing I don't really like about living here is that there are 80 people. It's too many. You have to wake up to the same faces every day. I'm looking forward to having some privacy!

Baby Love

Donna, 19

I've been homeless for roughly five months now, and when I first found myself with nowhere to live I was already seven months pregnant.

I had been living with my mum but we weren't getting on at all. She used to start arguments all the time and we used to clash. So, I started spending more and more time at my boyfriend's house and it got to the stage where I was just living there. Two years passed and then suddenly my boyfriend's mum told me to get out of her house. I would have moved out eventually anyway but the fact that she kicked me out when I was pregnant hurt and confused me. I suppose it just shows you what some people are like.

Anyway, I got over it. A friend let me stay with her until I could find something else, then someone told me to go to the council. They found me a place here, in a hostel for young women, including other women with babies. You're only supposed to live here for six months, but you can stay longer if you've got nowhere else to go.

What I really want is a place of my own. It's not bad here, but I like to keep myself to myself and sitting in your room looking at four walls all day can get depressing. The rooms are small and there's a kitchen area in each one but it means that your room smells of whatever you've cooked, so it puts you off a bit. But I can't complain; it's a roof over my head and the people are all right.

When I got my first contractions I was with my boyfriend and he drove me to the hospital. I was in labour for 23 hours, and it was very painful, but my sister and my boyfriend stayed with me the whole time. In the end I had to have a Caesarean because my baby was big: 8lbs 12 oz. I was awake for the operation and they put up a big light so I could see what was going on but it made me feel sick and I couldn't watch. My boyfriend wasn't much help either; he found it too scary!

It's funny but, when you have a baby, even if it's your first, you know what to do immediately. It's like an instinct, it just comes naturally. But I don't mind people advising me about my baby as much as they want, either. I think it's nice that they want to help; after all, you will make mistakes, no one's perfect. But there is a difference between advice and someone telling you what to do. It is so annoying when people just sit there and constantly say, 'Don't do that', 'Don't do this'. It's my daughter, not their's! My boyfriend's mum even tried to tell me not to get my own little girl's ears pierced.

It can be hard when the baby starts crying, but she's my responsibility and I can take care of her. She wasn't planned, but I'm really glad I had her. It has made my life better – apart from all the crying and the sleepless nights!

I would like to go back to work. I had a job in a bingo hall but what I'd really like to do is go back to college and do a secretarial course. It's only 16 hours a week and starts in September. If I can do something like that, I'll be able to get another job and that means I can start looking for a flat.

The only thing that worries me is leaving my daughter with somebody else. I don't want to do that because even when I leave her with someone for an hour I miss her. And I don't think anyone can look after her as well as I do because I know everything about her. But if you want to go out and earn money you've got to do it.

I would like to have another baby so that my daughter isn't an only child but I want to wait until I am in my 20s; say, around 27. It would be nice to have a little boy.

Occasionally I see my mum now and since I've moved out of her house the relationship has been a thousand times better. Living on my own means I haven't got anyone nagging me, I can just chill out. My boyfriend's mum even lets me stay on the odd night, too, if it's too late to come home, and she let me stay there for a couple of days to relax after the birth.

If someone wants to move out just for the sake of moving out and getting their own place, my advice would be to stay at home as long as you can. It's expensive to move out, especially if you've got children. On the other hand no one should have to go through what I went through or put up with being treated badly.

I want my daughter to grow up feeling that she can talk to me as a friend, as well as a mother, and I will listen. The relationship between me and my mum was bad. I'll do anything I can to prevent things getting like that between me and my child.

Beside the Sea

Sonia, 17

I was 16 and studying for my exams when I first started drinking. Just hanging around with mates and having a good time. But when I finished my exams I began to drink much more heavily. I felt I'd really let my parents down, so I left home.

Having nowhere to live, I slept at friends' houses or behind the local day centre. I hung around with other homeless people in the town centre and continued to drink heavily, but I was beginning to realise that it was too much. I asked one of the staff at the day centre for help and ended up going to stay at one of my mum's friends' houses. That was the same day I met Neil.

Neil was a homeless man who was travelling around from town to town. He was unlike anybody I had ever known. He spoke *to* me, not *at* me, and he made me laugh. Neil asked if I wanted to go to Brighton to make a fresh start. I agreed and we left the next day.

In our new town I met many homeless people and became friends with a lot of them. Life on the streets was a lot harder than I'd imagined it to be, and within a few days of arriving, we had all our bags stolen, including all of our personal possessions and our sleeping bags. That meant we had to sleep under the catamarans on the beach without any covers until we managed to get some more bedding.

We made a little money from begging, but most of the time this was used to buy drink. As a way of making more money, we began selling *The Big Issue*. With more money coming in we could start to replace the things that had been stolen.

After about a month of sleeping on the beach or in subways when it rained, Neil and I moved into a beach hut. OK, so there was no heating or electricity, but it was a roof and four walls and it gave us a bit of privacy at last.

On Neil's birthday, we got married in a traveller's wedding ceremony, where we had to jump over a broom. All our new friends were there and it was a good day.

Then, at 6 a.m. one morning, the police decided to evict us from the beach hut, so we found ourselves back on the beach for a few weeks. After that we moved into a squat that had heating and electricity and a little bit of furniture. This was the best place we had stayed in so far.

About three months after arriving in Brighton, I went to the day centre and saw the nurse for a pregnancy test. It was positive. I hadn't used contraceptives, even though you can get them from drop-in centres if you're homeless. I don't know why I didn't use them. Maybe it was just the last thing on my mind. When you're homeless, you have to think about the basics: where you're going to sleep, how you're going to eat.

Anyway, the nurse gave me a letter to take to the council stating I was pregnant. Within two hours of going to their offices, we were given a bedsit. The staff at *The Big Issue* office helped me to get registered with a doctor and we got a vendors' support-fund grant to buy some essential items for the bedsit.

From then on, things began to look up for us. I gave up drinking for my unborn baby's sake and, shortly afterwards, Neil also decided to stop. After being in the bedsit for about five weeks we were given a one-bedroom flat with a shared toilet and bathroom. However, this was only temporary.

I decided to write to my parents for the first time since leaving home, to tell them that I was OK and that I was pregnant. Neil kept telling me to write, but I was worried. But a few days later, a letter arrived from my mum and, to my surprise, she was congratulating me and Neil and inviting us to stay for Christmas.

Then, just before Christmas, we received an eviction notice, stating that we had four weeks to find alternative accommodation. The council said we had made ourselves intentionally homeless, because I had left home and Neil had kept a dog in his last place without permission from the landlord.

We were devastated. We tried to get help from *The Big Issue* staff and other people. We knew that if we didn't find another place, we would be forced to live on the beach again. Thankfully we were offered a permanent flat, and we jumped at the chance.

We went away to my parents and had a good time, not

having to worry about our accommodation. When we returned we were told we could go and see the flat. It was a one-bedroom ground-floor flat. *The Big Issue* helped us get grants and loans from social services. We moved in and set about making the place look as nice as possible.

That was about five months ago, and now we are all quite settled. Toni Ann, our daughter, was born on the 16th May. I know that we're going to have to move again when Toni is older, but I'm sure we will always be able to sort something out.

I think it's weird to compare my life when I first came to Brighton, with little more than the clothes I stood up in, to where I am today. Now I have a husband, a young baby, two dogs and a flat.

But for anyone thinking of deliberately becoming homeless or running away from home, I would say, think very hard before you do so. It may seem great to start with, having no one to tell you what to do all the time, but after a while it can be a nightmare. After all, not everyone is as lucky as I was.

On My Own Two Feet

Sally, 18

I left home when I turned 16. My mum hit the bottle because my nan died, and she kept rowing with my stepfather. Mum was always out and me and my sister Susan, who was two years younger, had to look after our four brothers and sisters. I had no freedom in my life. I was getting the hump so quickly before I left because I felt under so much pressure, and I started taking it out on the little 'uns, shouting at them. I never hit them – I don't believe in hitting children – but I felt bad.

Mum did drink before my nan died, but not as much as she did afterwards. Nan got ill after Grandad died. It was terrible; I found him dead at the top of the stairs. After that, Nan started going in and out of hospital. She died in my arms. The hospital said it was because she had something wrong with her lungs, but I think she died of a broken heart.

I was very close to my nan. My mum says that when I was born, she didn't want me because she was only 18 years old, but my nan told her she wasn't getting rid of me and Nan used to look after me a lot herself. When Nan died, everything went downhill for me.

I'd been looking after the four children since the youngest was aged three. When I left, they were aged 11, 10, 9 and 7. Everywhere I went, I had to bring them with me. I had to take them to school, pick them up, clean them, feed them, dress them. Susan and I had to do it all. My youngest sister even grew up calling me 'Mum' because she honestly believed that I was her mother. It was hard for me to tell her I wasn't, I was her big sister.

It also meant I was forever bunking off school. I think it was because I never had any free time at home. I missed a lot of schooling, but the school wanted me to go back and do my GCSEs; they said they would take my 'situation' into consideration. In the end, I passed them all – I don't know how!

It was really difficult for me to leave my brothers and sisters, and Susan, behind. Susan wanted to come with me because she didn't like Mum's drinking, either. I was so used to looking after the children, it felt as if they were being taken away from me. But my boyfriend couldn't hack it anymore, with me always having to do everything for the kids. He kept telling me that I had to get out of the situation I was in: he could see what it was doing to me. In the end, he gave me an ultimatum: leave now, or lose him. All the other boyfriends I'd ever had had left me because of the situation at home. I said to myself, I'm not losing this one, and four years down the line, I'm still with the same guy.

I met my boyfriend through my cousin and I've known him since I was eight or nine. We met up a couple of months after my nan died. We started talking and we got on really well. Then we started seeing each other. Before I met him, he was in and out of prison all the time for stealing cars. I've got him out of that. He's got a clean licence now. He treats me well; he's never laid a finger on me.

I knew that if I left, Mum would have to look after the kids herself and it would help her give up drinking. I was working with a friend in a shop at the time and I just thought, That's it, I'm going. At the time my mum kept saying, 'If you want to go, go.' I'd already run away four times when I was 15, but I'd always come back, so I suppose Mum thought it would be the same this time. It wasn't. One day after work, I just didn't go home.

For two years I stayed on people's floors and once I went to a homeless hostel, but I only stayed there for two days because I didn't like it and my boyfriend couldn't stay with me. At first Mum couldn't find me but then she found out where I was staying and started giving me hassle, saying she was going to belt me. She kept phoning when she was drunk so I had to go to a solicitor. They wrote a letter telling her I'd take action if she didn't stop. She had even started cashing my giros.

It was my boyfriend and my cousin who finally persuaded me to go to the council homeless unit and ask for a place. I had no confidence; I'd never lived on my own and was missing my brothers and sisters. I thought I wouldn't be able to cope if I didn't have other people around me.

At the time my boyfriend was living at his mum's and he always came to see me wherever I was staying. He said he wanted to be with me and that we needed to find somewhere where we could live together. Eventually the council offered me a one-bedroom flat.

I remember the first time I walked into my flat. It was empty and I panicked. I thought, How am I going to build this up? I've got nothing. I put in for a social security loan and they refused, saying I wasn't getting enough benefit to pay it back. So I went to social services and my social worker wrote to charities to get me things.

I'm in a tower block on the fourth floor. I like the flat, but not the estate. Drug addicts sit on the stairs, which means you're frightened to go down them. They also knock on the door at 4 a.m., asking for spoons to help them take their drugs. I just tell them where to go.

To tell the truth, at first I was scared to have a flat. I didn't know how to build stuff into it, how to pay the rent, how to run a home. But now I can run it quite easily. I feel a lot more independent, standing on my own two feet at last.

By the time I got the flat my mum was getting involved in my life again, saying she didn't like my boyfriend. Finally she left me alone and me and my boyfriend started living together. Nine months later I discovered I was pregnant with my daughter. I was already four months gone when I found out. My mate had given me a settee and there was no one to help me get it home, so I dragged it all the way from one block of flats to another. All of a sudden I started bleeding, as though I was having a period. I went to the clinic and they told me I was pregnant. I was very happy; I knew I

71

would be a good mother.

I'd had a lot of problems when I was younger, but moving out and getting a place of my own changed me. Before, if anyone said the wrong thing, I used to rear up. I couldn't seem to control my temper and I kept getting into fights. I even got done for actual bodily harm once because I got into a fight when I was sticking up for my brothers and sisters. The police told me to stay out of trouble and I didn't get charged. My boyfriend could tell you how I used to be; I used to beat him up when I first left the children behind. He said I needed counselling to control my temper. When I found out about the baby, I calmed down. I knew if I kept on fighting I would only end up in prison.

Moving out also changed things with my mum and we're on better terms now. When I left she hit the bottle more, but by now she had slowed right down. The Christmas after I moved out, I went round with presents for my brothers and sisters and about a month later I phoned and said I thought it was time to bury the hatchet. We talked and things seemed to get better after that. She promised faithfully that if I kept in contact with her she would stop drinking. She has a drink maybe once a week now, and she's moved house away from all her drinking friends, so she's out of harm's way.

I know I won't regret my decision to keep my baby. My daughter is eight weeks old now and I wouldn't give her up for anything. When I first discovered I was pregnant, I told my boyfriend that I didn't want to have a baby that couldn't have its father around or was brought up without any money. He said he wouldn't ever go; he'd stick around and would come and see her every day, even if things didn't work out between him and me.

I don't want my daughter to have the life I've had. I want her to have a better life, to be able to come to me with a problem. The flat isn't ideal for someone with a baby because of the drug addicts, but at least my baby has freedom within her own home. More than anything else, I want her to have a childhood. I didn't have one. I never knew what it was like to be a child. The way I look at it, it's my responsibility to look after her, not the other way round.

Sister Act

Susan (Sally's sister), 17

When I was about 13 or 14, my mum turned to drink and used to go out to pubs, leaving me and Sally to babysit her four children. When Mum and my stepdad were drunk they used to fight, and the children would start screaming. It was a bad atmosphere. I hated it.

Me and Sally didn't have any time to ourselves so we used to bunk off school a lot. I didn't get any qualifications; I'd missed so much, it wasn't worth me going back to get any exams.

Sally left when she was 16. She only told me she was going; she didn't tell anyone else. We used to run away all the time because we didn't want to look after the kids. We wanted our freedom just like anyone else of our age, but Mum wouldn't have it.

After Sally left, things just got worse. Sometimes Mum wouldn't even come home at night and I had to take the kids to school, bring them home, cook for them and put them to bed. There was no one I could speak to about it.

Eventually, after about a year, I decided to go, too. I was 16 now and Mum couldn't stop me. I went to my real father's and stayed there for about a year. My mum and my stepdad kept telling him to throw me out. They said they never wanted me back, but they didn't want me at his place, either. Then my dad did a burglary and a robbery, both whilst he was drinking, and he got caught and sent to prison. He's in prison now. My stepfather got hold of the keys to his place, came round, put all my stuff out in the street and changed the locks.

After that I stayed at my boyfriend's sister's place for a bit, then at my sister's. Then I slept on friends' floors, and even in a caravan in someone's garden for two months. By that time it was November and I'd discovered I was pregnant. It was winter and far too cold for a pregnant woman to stay in a caravan.

I got so sick of it all that Sally took me to the council homeless unit and they put me in a hostel. I asked to be put in the same one that she had once stayed in, but because I hadn't run away in that area they said they couldn't do that. Finally in March, because of my pregnancy, I got a place in a family hostel. I had a room and had to pay rent out of £29-a-week benefits. (I wasn't 18 yet so I wasn't entitled to any more.) By the time I bought food and paid the rent, the money was gone.

The hostel was for men and women with kids. The people below me were always rowing whenever the man got drunk. You could tell he was drunk from the way his speech was slurred. There was a Spanish lady next door and she told me she had seen him come up and knock on my door at night. I hadn't ever heard him. That was scary, especially because I was there on my own.

Then one day I got a letter to say I'd been given a two-bedroom council flat. I love it. It's really nice and it's quiet. I'm round the corner from where I'm going to have the baby and my boyfriend's living with me. Sally's helped me a lot and has given me some baby stuff.

She has had her baby and I'm due in seven weeks. We can do what we want now. We aren't being told what to do or who to look after, so we can make our own lives, have our own families.

I still see my brothers and sisters. Sometimes they come and stay at my house, one at a time. I can't afford to go and see my dad in prison because of living on £29 a week, but I do write to him and I will let him see the baby when it's born.

I speak to my mum now, because she doesn't drink anymore – well, she can't, there's no one else to look after the kids – but I'll only see her in our local day centre. I think overall it was a good idea for me and Sally to run away. It helped Mum realise that she's got children to look after and she can't keep dumping them on everybody else.

I still can't forgive my mum and stepdad for what they've done to me. I do talk to them and I'll let them see my baby when he or she is born, but I won't let them rule me or my child. I don't want Mum to get involved. I'll see her but that's as far as it goes. And having seen what drink's done to them I won't drink; I hate drink now. I'm not going to end up like my mum.

Drugs Don't Work

Estella, 19

I grew up in a small Spanish village in an area that is very popular with tourists. I didn't like it; it was a very commercial place and the people were so materialistic. If you wanted to go out, there were only discos with techno music, which were full of people on holiday. I just didn't see any future for me there. The only jobs you could get were all connected with the tourist industry: in shops, restaurants, bars and hotels and even if you went to university it was difficult to get anything interesting. I had been studying so hard and was so stressed out I just needed a break.

I'd visited London before and I really liked the way of life, so I decided I would come here and try to get a job. When I first arrived I did have some money. I was on my own and I went to the cheapest hotel I could find, which was £15 a night. I started looking for work but my money ran out before I could find anything.

I started going to Leicester Square and met other homeless people there. We became friends and used to hang around together. We all slept in doorways there and it made me feel safer to be with other people who were in the same position.

It was OK at first because it was summer, so not too cold, and we could go to a day centre to have a shower and clean up.

One thing that annoyed me was tourists trying to take photos of us as we slept. We used to tell them to go away or give us some money; they weren't treating us with respect. Once I was asleep and a man came with a big TV camera and started filming me and my friend. We asked him what he was doing and he said, 'Don't worry. This is for Spanish television.' I was so angry. 'What?' I screamed, 'Go away!' I didn't want my mother to turn on her TV and see a picture of me sleeping on the streets. I phone my family every Sunday and eventually I did tell them I had slept rough, but I never told them I'd had to beg. They would have been so disappointed.

What I found most depressing about being homeless was the problem with drugs and alcohol; there are loads of people dying on the streets. I don't abuse drugs or alcohol; I get drunk sometimes and take a trip once every two or three months, but I'm not dependent on anything apart from cigarettes.

In Spain I never knew anyone who died from drugs but now I know quite a few – not close friends but people I used to see around every day. You'd wake up in the morning and someone would say, 'Do you remember this person or that person? Well, they've died.' They were mostly young, between 20 and 30, and most of the time it was through an overdose.

I'm proud I didn't get into drugs when I was on the streets. It would have been so easy to do. I hate seeing people waking up shaking, just because they need some alcohol or drugs. I'm embarrassed when I have no money and have to beg a cigarette; I can't imagine what it must be like to go begging to get crack or heroin.

When the weather turned cold I stayed in lots of places. At first I was in a squat and had a bedroom with some friends. Then I went to a women's refuge, which had no bedrooms, just cubicles, and where you could hear everyone snoring all night. After a while the hostel kicked me out because housing benefit weren't paying the rent. I made a claim for benefits in October but I didn't get any money until February, I don't know how I survived all that time. Sometimes I had to sleep on the streets and it was so cold I would wake up shaking and couldn't stop.

Now I have my own flat. It took me about three months to get it and I've been living there for three weeks. It takes a while to get used to living on your own because when you are on the streets there are always lots of people around, but I'm managing.

Next month I am starting a course for sound engineering on the New Deal and I hope to be able to get a job in a recording studio. I think music was one of the reasons I chose to come to London. I love all kinds of guitar music – rock, punk, heavy metal – and I'd heard about London through the punk scene. Nobody is into that kind of music where I come from and I couldn't find anyone to start a band with. I would like to be in one here but someone stole my electric guitar in the last hostel I stayed in.

I still go back to Leicester Square to see the people I know but I don't like it; I find it depressing now.

In five years time I hope that I will be working in a job I like and that I'll be good at what I do. Maybe I'll even have my own band!

Just Listen

Ceri, 17

When I stayed on the streets for the first time I was with a friend. We slept on this dirty, wet, ripped old sofa inside the communal area of a block of flats. We were freezing cold, tired and hungry, but we had no choice.

The second time I slept on the streets I was on my own. I was so scared. I didn't really know what to do at first and I just walked around for ages. But then it got so cold I had to find somewhere, so I crawled into this little shed thing by the side of a block of flats. I was freezing but eventually I fell asleep. In the morning I was woken up when this old lady walked in. She started screaming and ran off to her own flat. I didn't hang around. I just got up and went straight to my friend's house. I'd been dying to go to the toilet all night, but I wasn't prepared to go in a bush or anything like that.

*

I started running away from home when I was 14. My mum had found a new boyfriend who was 18, only a few years older than me, and I didn't like him. We argued all the time about different things. The house didn't feel like home anymore.

I used to stay out until all hours. Mum kept hassling me but I didn't listen to a word she said. The police were always looking for me and as soon as they found me, they'd take me straight back home. But it was no good; I'd just leave again as soon as I could.

My friend and I used to run away together because she was having problems with her parents, too. We'd go out and sleep anywhere we could find.

One time we ran away and went to her nan's house. Just as we were about to eat our dinner, there was a knock at the door. It was the police. They took me home yet again. Mum was furious and we had a huge argument. I said to her, 'You either choose me or him.' Mum started crying and said, 'I'm not going to choose.' She didn't seem to hear what I was saying; I just wanted her to realise how unhappy I was. But she wouldn't listen, so I just picked up my clothes and left.

After that I stayed at my friend's nan's for a bit, then I went to stay with my father. He was a heavy drinker and every night I would go home and find him drunk, stumbling about the place and falling over. So, in the end, I ran away from there as well.

That night I couldn't find anywhere to stay, so I had to sleep on the streets again. It was the same the next night, and the next. I ended up sleeping on the streets for about two weeks until this lady I used to babysit for asked me where I was saying. She'd guessed I was sleeping rough and I told her she was right. So she phoned the local social services and they told her to call the police. 'Why should I phone the police?' she said 'she hasn't done anything wrong.' The social services' reply was to tell her to put me back out on the streets. She was fuming. 'If I put her back on the streets and she gets hurt or killed, then it will be on my conscience.' With that, she slammed down the phone. Five minutes later she called them back and said, 'If you do not come and help this child, then I will go to the local newspaper. You are supposed to be there for children but you won't even help.' That worked; a social worker came round within half an hour.

The lady said to her husband that if it was OK with him, I could stay and live with them. He had a little think and said yes. The social worker gave them some money for me, left, and that was the last I saw of him.

I lived with that couple for about a year and a half, but I was still getting into a bit of trouble. I hadn't really sorted myself out, so I left and went to stay with another friend. I started to shoplift to get food and clothes, but I was caught. I had to go to the police station and they gave me a caution.

Six months later I was homeless again. The woman I was living with at the time was a junkie, and she got sent to prison. So I went back to live with another friend for a while. I decided I had to find something a bit more permanent, so I went with a friend to the council housing office and they put us in a B&B. It was full of junkies and people who were in trouble with the police. The only good thing was that at least my friend was there, too.

When we walked in, there was this disgusting smell. It

was so bad I was heaving and I thought I was going to be sick. We were waiting for 20 minutes before the manager appeared. He took us to the office to get the keys to our room, but we discovered that he'd given us two single rooms. I told him that we were supposed to have a room together but he said that the social worker had told him to put us in separate ones. I don't know what had happened, but when you're staying in a place like that, you want to be with your friends. The manager told us we could sleep in each other's rooms and that's what we decided to do.

We went up to have a look at them and couldn't believe our eyes when we opened the door. They were like prison cells, stinking and dirty. The locks were broken so someone only had to push the door to get in. They were disgusting.

That night the manager asked us if we wanted to be woken up for breakfast. We said yes. But no one ever knocked on our door and when we finally woke up it was 10.30 and we'd missed breakfast. For the rest of the day we didn't have any food. We were so hungry.

The people in the B&B were very rough. When we went out of the room into the corridor the first night, there was a gang of people and some of them were drinking and drug dealing, so we just went back into our rooms and cleaned up.

All night people kept running in and out and we couldn't sleep. The next day in the telly room, some people were going on about things being pinched from their rooms. My friend said that if anything was pinched from our room, there'd be murder. In a place like that you have to stick up for yourself.

But the final straw came later that day. This boy from

our B&B went down to another hostel and put a gun to another guy's head. It was all over some girl, but that did it for me. I went back to the council housing unit and told them there was no way I was staying there.

At the moment I am staying anywhere I can find until the council rehouse me, but that could take a while so I have to wait. At least I get Jobseekers' Allowance and hardship allowance now, which is £77.80 a fortnight. Before that I had to shoplift; I didn't like it, but I had to do it in order to survive.

To get the allowances I had to go to a careers service. Because I was homeless, I'd lost out on my education and hadn't been able to do any exams. So my career worker put me on a project and sent me to a training agency, but they said I couldn't start until I had a permanent address, so again I had to wait.

I've never had anyone I can really talk to about my problems apart from my friends. When I was on the streets, social services were no good. I don't know why they even bothered; they were no help to me. But now I can go over to my local community centre and talk to one of the youth workers and I know they will listen. For me, that's a very important thing.

Freedom to Choose

Layla, 19

I am Moroccan. I came here for a holiday and decided to stay. I felt I had no future at home; I couldn't go to college, I couldn't work, I just had to stay at home because my father was a bit too strict. I wanted to be free. I was growing up and my father did not like it at all when I stood up to him. Once he even said that he would give me away to the first man who came knocking at the door, just to get rid of me. I don't know whether he meant it or was just saying it because he was angry, but it made me suspicious. Arranged marriages still happen in Morocco and I didn't want to be given away to someone I'd never even seen before.

Most of my friends had a bit of freedom and that made it worse for me. My parents wouldn't let me go out with them without taking my older sister. I hated it – it really used to get to me.

It's hard to get a visa to visit any European country if you are a young Moroccan because the authorities are worried that you will pretend you are going on holiday and not come back. But it doesn't surprise me that people do try and run away, because the treatment some of us get isn't very fair. If you are beaten up by your father and you report it to the police, for example, they just say he's your father and he has the right to punish you. Punish you maybe, but not throw you all over the place.

My father used to beat all seven of us. His father used to beat him very badly, so I suppose he was taking it out on us. I am the youngest and all my sisters and brothers had left home young, got married and run off to different countries in Europe. My brother went to England and that was why I first came here.

My dad managed to get a visa and decided that he, my mum and I would all go on holiday to visit my brother in London. I soon saw that a woman in Britain could have more freedom and a better lifestyle. I realised my family wasn't going to be around for ever – my father has cancer and my mother is ill – and I wanted to do something with my life. I knew it was up to me, while I was still young, because my brothers and sisters couldn't take me in. They had enough problems as it was.

My brother in London was no better than my dad. While I was staying with him, I was able to go to college because of my visa. Normally I always got home at 7.30 p.m. but one evening I was late because of the traffic and got back at 8 p.m. He picked up a knife and pointed it at me and my mum had to beg him on her knees to stop. I don't know why some men act like that. You can't sit and discuss it quietly; it always seems to end up in a fight. I used to answer my dad and my brother back and that just made them more angry. But if I know I'm right and the person accusing me is wrong, I have to tell them. My mum would never say anything against my dad and brother and it really used to get to me.

I got married to an Englishman just so that I could leave home. I met him by chance and was seeing him behind my parents' back. He knew they were strict so he proposed marriage to me. When I told my parents they were happy; it meant they were finally getting rid of me.

But three months down the line this man started to become violent. By this time my parents had gone home and I didn't have anyone to turn to. I knew that if I contacted my brother he would only blame me. One day my husband beat me up so badly after an argument, I realised I couldn't take it anymore. He kicked me out and told me to go home to Morocco.

By this time I had a job in a burger bar. Someone there let me stay with them for a while, but in the end I had to move on because someone else was moving into the flat. I also had to leave my job because I knew my husband would come looking for me there and I was afraid.

After that things got really rough. I didn't know anyone, I had nowhere to stay, no money, nothing. I had to sleep on the streets for three days with my six bags of belongings. It was horrible; people kept hassling me all the time. I was too ashamed and embarrassed to sleep in shop doorways, so I ended up sleeping in Regent's Park in the bushes, hiding from everyone. When anyone tried to talk to me I just pretended I couldn't speak English. I looked all scruffy and dirty because I couldn't go anywhere to clean myself properly.

I remember just sitting there and crying. I had no money and felt that my life was finished. I wished my parents had never brought me into this world or had killed me at birth if I was such a problem for them.

There was a woman there watching me as I sat crying. She started to talk to me and gave me some food. She was from Somalia but had become a British citizen. She was kind to me and is still a friend now. She made me stay at her place and took me to some hostels for the homeless to try and find somewhere more permanent to stay. It was very hard. No one wanted to take me because I couldn't claim benefits.

Eventually I managed to get into a hostel in central London. The people running it had to send me to social services to help me get money to stay there. They found me a social worker but she wasn't very nice. She kept asking me why I didn't go back to my own country. In the end I asked her if she was supposed to be helping me or just giving me more stress. Then social services gave me someone else to talk to and she was a very nice lady. I will never forget what she did for me. She sorted out my place in the hostel and managed to get me £50 to live on for the next two weeks. I was able to buy some food and I had to buy some cheap clothes because a girl at the hostel stole almost everything I had before she left.

At that time I wasn't allowed to work at all, so I had to hussle on the street. Some of us from the hostel used to steal clothes from shops and sell them to prostitutes in Soho. Some people called me a prostitute as well, but I didn't care. No one was going to put food in my tummy and I did what I had to to survive.

Soon I had to leave that hostel because four girls kept

threatening me. They hated me because I wouldn't talk to them. I moved to a shared house, which I thought was going to be better, but the nuns who ran it were racist. There were people from Africa and South America there and the nuns spoke Spanish, so whenever a charity box of clothes arrived, the head nun would call her favourites to choose what they wanted and all the black people had to take what was left.

The head nun always picked on me. When I went out she used to go to my room and snoop around. She was always asking if I'd been drinking or taking drugs, and she even threatened me with Immigration once. I pretended I didn't care and said, 'Great, call them,' but she really scared me. She shouldn't have done that; she was supposed to be there to help me, not threaten me.

I told my social worker what had happened and I was moved to the hostel I live in now. I don't like it, but it's a roof over my head. It's full of a mixture of people from different countries who have been transferred there by social services and local councils. Some of the men stare at me as if they have never seen a woman before and that makes me feel uncomfortable. The kitchen has cockroaches and I saw one of them run under my bed the other day, but otherwise I'm lucky. I have a single room with a shower and a TV. I've tried to make it look homely by putting some pictures on the wall, but I do miss home and wish that everything was better. At the moment, I am just coping.

I found a job working as a receptionist in a hair and beauty salon in Knightsbridge and it made me very happy, but I overslept one day and they sacked me. I still don't understand; everyone there liked me, I did my job properly, and I had always turned up on time apart from that one day.

Sometimes I'm scared by the thought that I might bump into my family on the street. I don't know what I would do – I think I'd just want to disappear. But from time to time I do think about going back to Morocco. I would have to have something to take back, like an education, because no one is going to look after me. I think that it would also be hard because I am used to my freedom now. I can be what I want to be and I've got the right to say what I want, so I don't think anyone would have me back home.

I love travelling and communicating with people, and I can speak four languages, so I would like to work in tourism. At the moment that is just a dream because I need to get qualifications and I'm not allowed to. I've got a work permit and I can claim benefits, but I need British citizenship to get an education. I'm waiting for the government to tell me what my status is and whether I'll be allowed to stay in the country or not. My solicitor keeps saying, 'If I get any news you'll be the first to hear,' but I've been waiting for a decision for three years now.

Other people are going off to university and I'm still at square one. I've been trying to go to university since I was 17 and now I'm 19. My life is going fast and I want to get up and *do* something.

At the moment I'm just looking for any job. I'm going crazy; I don't have any money and all I seem to be doing is getting up and going out of the hostel every morning, coming back at night and sleeping. It's seriously driving me mad. You're pushed around so many places when you are homeless that it becomes difficult to focus on anything. Someone offered me a job as a stripper the other day, but there's no way I'd take it. I may not have much else, but I will keep my dignity even if it means having no money.

It's My Life

Jenny, 16

I was 15 and living with my mum and dad when I found out that I was four months pregnant. It took a little while for me to take it in and then decide what I wanted to do, so I didn't tell my parents for about a month. They weren't too happy, to say the least. They are from China and are very strict. They were also unhappy because I was so young and hadn't finished school.

They agreed to let me stay at home until I had the baby, but after that I would have to leave. I stayed because I didn't have any other choice and, in their favour, they did treat me more like an adult during that time.

I had my baby daughter in hospital and my parents came to see her when she was born. But although she is their only grandchild, they stuck to their decision about throwing me out.

Thankfully my grandmother, who lives with my parents, called my elder sister and told her I had nowhere to stay, and my sister came and got me from the hospital. All I had with me was a suitcase with the things I'd needed there, so my sister had to go back home and get the rest of my stuff.

My sister is 23 and has no children yet. I managed to stay with her up until the baby was about four months old, but one of my other sisters was living in the flat and it only had two bedrooms, so things were getting a bit crowded. I went to the local housing unit for help and my health visitor also gave me some advice. That's how I got referred to the hostel I am in at the moment but I'm also on the housing list, waiting for a home of my own.

I'm hoping to get a place soon and I just take things one day at a time. I know the baby's father has been calling my parents to try to find out where I am but I'm not going to stay in touch with him. Things just weren't working out between me and him before I left.

The way I'm living now is so different to the way I lived before. I don't really have any family to talk to, although I do speak to people in the hostel. I'm quite shy, so it takes me a while to get to know someone properly.

My other friendships are drifting away because our lives have become so different. Basically, I have a baby and they don't, and that affects all sorts of things.

Having a baby is a strange experience. I had done some babysitting before and have lots of little cousins, so I suppose I was already used to young children.

My parents are all right about my daughter now, but they still think I'm too young to have a child of my own. I don't really see them or talk to them much, I just go back home to visit my sister and my grandmother.

In a way it does hurt me that my parents aren't very supportive but all the children in our family (I've got three sisters and one brother) don't really talk to them because they see things so differently. It could be because we grew up in Britain and they grew up in China. They wanted me to go to school and then on to university and end up with a good job. I don't want to do that anymore. I used to be very career orientated but having the baby changed me. Now I want to be a full-time mum and have other children so that my baby can have brothers and sisters to play with.

My parents would like me to marry someone of my own kind because they are very traditional, but it's not what I want at all. I suppose I had to move away to have the kind of life *I* wanted rather than the kind of life *they* wanted for me.

In the Deep End

Michelle, 16

I left home one November. I'd gone through Christmas at home before, and I couldn't face another one. I just didn't enjoy it. I used to sit there, not wanting to open my mouth in case I got shouted at by my mum, my brother or my sister. It was like they expected me to muck Christmas up.

I was always getting screamed at. I didn't really fit in at home and my mum yelled at me more than the others. I think it was because she thought I was the most mature and intelligent, even though I was the youngest. I was top of the top class at school and my brother was bottom of the bottom class. But my brother's not dumb and when it comes to rowing, he can hold his own.

I love swimming and my brother and I used to practise every day. But there were always arguments over it and in the end, my mum said I wasn't allowed to swim ever again. That's one of the reasons why I ran away from home the first time.

It was earlier in the year, when I'd just turned 15. I packed a bag, left the house, and rang a helpline number from a phone box. I was on the phone for about five hours. I don't want to write about everything my mum did but it's enough to say that I was very upset. Mum had a lot of money problems and I understand that, but it was really bad for me.

When I rang the helpline, the person on the end of the phone told me that because I was 15, I would have to go to social services. I rang them but the first thing they wanted to know was my name and address. I didn't want to give them that because they would contact my mum, so I hung up and called the helpline again. They gave me the address of one hostel and the telephone number for a service that helps you find a place. I had to lie and say I was 16, but the service did call me back and told me they'd got me a vacancy in Soho.

It was 9 p.m. and I was outside central London. I was very young and innocent – just getting the train to Kings Cross scared me. Soho was very frightening. I got lost and when I finally found the hostel, there were two drunks sitting outside on the steps. They said to me, 'It's a shithole in there, you don't want to go in.' I was so scared I could feel my heart banging in my chest. But in the end the hostel wasn't so bad.

The next day I went to a day centre, where I had to tell the staff my real age because they wanted me to get identification. The hostel was then told my age but agreed to keep me on until I got somewhere else to stay, and by that time I was only a few days off my 16th birthday.

I was really happy there; it was the best week of my life so far. I was poor, but free, and no one was having a go at me. For a while I felt I was really living my own life.

Then I found out that my mum had reported me missing. Pictures of me had been shown on local television and people I knew kept telling me they'd seen posters everywhere. I had to phone a friend at home to find out what was going on. She told me that my mum was devastated so I decided to phone her and tell her I was safe and well. I had left her a running-away letter so she knew why I had gone but she begged me to meet her anyway. She was crying non-stop. I didn't want to go back to the town I'd come from because I felt safe in central London so in the end Mum agreed to come to Kings Cross.

When I saw Mum I felt so guilty. She looked terrible: her face was all flushed and she looked like she was dying. No matter what, I still loved her, so I said I would come home. But I'd changed; I wasn't going to take all the screaming anymore. I told her what she'd been doing to me, how it had affected me. Only later did I realise she hadn't really taken in what I'd said.

I'd made a lot of friends at the hostel and I wanted to say goodbye to them all, even though my mum said they were 'lower people'. They had helped and supported me and there was no way I was just getting on a train without seeing them first.

I went back to the hostel and said goodbye to all my friends. I have kept in contact with some of them ever since. It was a mixed hostel for long-term homeless people and they made me feel so welcome. There was one girl in particular who scared me at first, but once we got chatting I realised she was really nice. We always had a brilliant time together, just doing simple things like walking up Oxford Street, laughing and having fun. We had to leave the hostel at 8 a.m. every day and not return until 8 p.m., which is hard when you've nothing else to do and no money, but me and my friends knew we could depend on each other.

I hadn't been home for long before things got bad again. By November I decided I couldn't take it any more, so I went back to see a worker at the day centre I used to go to the first time I'd run away. She was the first person I'd really talked to about home face to face. It had been so hard for me but eventually everything had come out. When I went back to see her this time, I still couldn't look her in the eye. She was the only person I'd ever told everything to.

It's weird. Whatever happened I would always defend my mum because I felt so much respect for her. It didn't matter what she did, I would think of an excuse for her because she's my mum and I love her. But she also scared me. When I told the worker about my decision to go back, get my bag, and tell my mum I was leaving, she thought I would be too afraid to do it. But I was 16 now, and Mum couldn't stop me.

When I told her, she was devastated. Everyone in the family kept steaming in and out of the room, having a go at me and trying to make me feel guilty. But I didn't want to be pressured any more – I was leaving, no matter what they said. As I put my bag on my shoulder and walked out of the door, I was shaking.

Mum put me back on the missing persons register, but this time I was able to call them and say I was 16, and didn't want to be found.

*

I didn't contact Mum for six months after that, apart from the one time when I went to get the rest of my stuff. I did ring my brother about a month later, knowing that Mum would be at work. I missed him a lot; it wasn't so bad at first, but after a while I needed to see him. I waited outside our school and we spent about 20 minutes together. We were both crying and it didn't go too well. Although I wanted to see him again, I decided to leave it for the moment because I knew he'd have to lie to the family and I didn't want him to get in trouble with Mum.

Then, about seven weeks ago, I picked up the phone and called her. I'd been with a friend who also didn't speak to her mum for about a year, and somehow I suddenly didn't feel as bad about Mum as I used to. I just felt content. I could also see Mum's point of view. She hadn't heard from me for so long, and I was so young. When I rang her we were on the phone for about an hour and a half. I went and visited her and also went back to the swimming class, which I hadn't been to for eight months. Now I go every week.

Because of leaving home, I didn't get to do my GCSEs, so I'm going back to college in September. I've been told by the resettlement team at my hostel that I should get a place in a shared flat in five months time. Mum still wants me to move back with her, but I can't. I think she knows I'm not coming back. I do visit her two or three times a week, but I go when I want, and leave when I want. It's not easy leaving home when you are young and I still have trouble dealing with things, but I have two lives now and if there is a problem with one, I've got the other one to go to. I like it; it gives me a sense of security.

Telling the Truth

Salina, 19

At the age of three months I was given away to my aunt and uncle, who live in the Philippines. They could not have children but my aunt had pretended she was pregnant, so the lie just got bigger and bigger. That is why my parents gave me away, to cover up the truth.

All the time I lived in the Philippines I really believed that my aunt and my uncle were my real parents. Then, when I was eight years old, my aunt finally did get pregnant and had a baby boy, so I was sent back to my family in Britain. It was so confusing for me; I saw these people I didn't even know saying to me, 'Come to mummy, come to daddy'. I felt lonely, isolated and afraid. And because I had lived away from them for so much of my early life, my parents never really treated me like a daughter.

Back 'home' I was sent to one school, then another,

where I was severely bullied. There was one girl in particular who was sick in the head and who tried to feed me maggots. She ended up being expelled. But the bullying made me late home from school and my mother thought I was up to something else. By the age of 12, I was already being called a slag by my own mother.

I left school at 14 and started working in the family business. I would get up at 6 a.m., work in the shop until 9 a.m., then go on to our post office, where I would finish at 5.30 p.m. After that I would go to Maths and English GCSE classes at college between 7.15 and 9.15 p.m. I didn't get good results and my dad hit me for that.

My parents are Sikh and in our culture women are not supposed to go out, cut our hair, eat meat, smoke or talk to outsiders. I did all that; I was a rebel! But then Mum found out that I was smoking and stealing cigarettes from our shop to sell to my friends. My parents also got it into their heads that I was sleeping with a Muslim friend of mine. They thought all sort of horrible things about me – that I was pregnant, that I was taking drugs – and so they made plans to send me to India to be married off.

My dad raped me for the first time just before I went. It was the night he returned from his father's funeral in India and I had phoned him from college to ask if he was OK (my parents had separated so I thought I should check on him). I could hear music in the background, laughing and joking, and my dad sounded as if he had been drinking. You wouldn't have thought he'd just been to a funeral.

I told him that I would go round after college. When I got to the house my little brother, who was nine, was also there and so was my uncle. My dad told me he had a beautiful dress for me upstairs. There's a Punjabi song about a beautiful dress and it's my favourite, so I went straight upstairs to look for it. I couldn't find it at first, then I saw it laid out on the bed. My dad came after me and shut the door. I asked, 'Is this mine?' but he just started touching my face and my breasts. Then he raped me. That was it.

Because I had been missing for about half an hour and because he had seen my dad closing the door, my little brother decided to come into the bedroom. He was horrified.

As soon as it was over I told my brother to get his stuff and we just started running. I didn't even know where we were running to; I just wanted to get as far away from that house as possible.

We went to my mum's house and my brother and I both told her what had happened. She didn't want to believe us, even though my brother kept saying, 'Believe her, she's telling the truth. Dad strangled her, Dad took her clothes off.' Mum just hit him and accused him of lying. Mum phoned Dad and asked him to come round to where she lived the next day. When he came, my dad tried to give me £50 to shut me up.

After that he just kept coming to Mum's house as if nothing had happened. I asked Mum not to leave me on my own with him and all she said was, 'Look, he's your father.' My brother was very good to me; he tried to look after me but he was very young, so there wasn't much he could do. I couldn't leave the business, either. No one believed me because my dad knew lots of influential people and was well regarded.

★

I was 14 when I was sent to India and I had no idea that I was being married off to a man of 40. The only reason I managed to get out of it was because my cousin there took pity on me and said I was too young. If he hadn't, I'd be married with lots of children by now. A lot of the men I saw out there drink a lot and all they want out of a woman is sex. There were little children of about nine with tiny children of their own. I found it very shocking.

When I got back from India I discovered my father had sold half my gold jewellery and a solid gold bangle, a family heirloom handed down from his great grand-father, to pay for my dowry.

Another thing I found when I returned was that my mother was covered in bruises, and I knew that my father had beaten her. I wanted to get straight back in the taxi and go round to shout at him.

It was shortly after my return that I got malaria. Mum came to visit me in the hospital and guess what she brought with her? Clean clothes, grapes, some books or magazines? No: she brought some paperwork from the business. Again, she'd thought the worst of me and imagined I was in hospital because I was pregnant or had AIDS.

I realised I couldn't go on at home and told a friend that I wanted to run away (although I didn't feel able to tell him about the rape). He got in touch with social workers but when we went to their office my dad was sitting there waiting for me. I couldn't believe it. I was told I had to go home because my parents were my legal guardians. He played on their sympathy by saying he was ill – Dad always wants sympathy from people – and he kept comparing me to my other two sisters, saying, 'What is wrong with this child?' The social workers fell for it.

I still have nightmares about what my dad did to me and I wake up crying and screaming. I've tried counselling but it's not helping at all. I got so depressed I even walked out into the middle of a busy road to try and kill myself. But nine months ago I finally managed to leave.

I knew I was going to make a move. I saw my brother just before I went off to college that day and I said goodbye to him. I'd planned to go clubbing with friends and I just didn't go back home. The next night I went clubbing again and I met the brother of a friend of mine, who was really nice. He said he could help me and he did – even though his mother already had ten children of her own, she took me in and was there for me when I needed her.

But I knew I couldn't stay there for ever so I went to a council homelessness unit. The man there said he couldn't do anything for me but I had my own list of hostels and was able to do a ring-round using their phone. Finally, at midnight, I managed to find a place in a hostel in Kings Cross.

It was hell – the place was full of prostitutes taking drugs. Luckily I didn't have to spend much of my time there because I found some work. I stayed for three months, then got thrown out because I was away babysitting for five days and hadn't cleared it with anyone first.

I met my current boyfriend at an underground station. After I was thrown out of the hostel, I stayed with him until I found somewhere else to live. He was really good to me – gave me food, somewhere to sleep and rang round hostels for me. In fact, he was the one who gave me the number of the hostel I'm living in at the moment.

All I ever wanted was tender loving care, but I never felt loved until I met him. He knows immediately when something's wrong. I can smile and laugh but he knows if I'm thinking something different. When I'm with him I don't have nightmares and I don't think too much about the past, but when I'm alone, all the rubbish in my head comes crowding in. I try to block it out by listening to music on my walkman but it doesn't always help. There are marks on me that I just can't wash away.

Recently my family found out where I live. A guy from home saw me walking down the street near here and he must have passed on the information to my parents. I've had letters from my mum and sister trying to make me feel guilty so that I will go home. They've used all sorts of stories to try and persuade me to come back. They told me that one of my sisters had taken drugs and had to go to hospital to have her stomach pumped, because I left home. Then Mum told me she had breast cancer. Dad even paid one of my friends to ring me and tell me he'd passed away, all so that I would return to the family. They'll be telling me something has happened to my little brother next – they've already told him that I'm dead. It sounds like they really want me back but I think all they want is someone to help them run the business. They've asked me how I can possibly live in a hostel with black people but my friends here have helped me more than my family ever did.

I'm scared that if my dad finds me here, he'll try to get me married off, so I've got the police involved. If he does come near me I'll press charges. I still don't understand why he did what he did to me and I worry about my brother. I want him to be in a safe environment and I don't think my father is safe at all.

But it hasn't stopped me getting on with my life. I've got two job offers so I'll be making some money soon. I'm really hard-working and like to keep myself busy – one day, I can see myself having my own business.

On a personal level I have started to open up and talk about things more. I've realised that if you hide from painful memories they just get worse, so you're only hurting yourself. I have learnt from what happened to me. If I ever have a family of my own, I want to make sure that my husband doesn't hit the children or drink too much because I know from personal experience that hitting and drinking can lead to something much, much worse.

A Travelling Man

Beth, 18

I hardly got any sleep last night. Dan and I were just getting our heads down in a car park after a long day when the sodding security guard came and told us to shift quick smart, or the Old Bill would be called. Charming! We'd been there for the past three weeks and everything had been hunky dory. Then along comes this guard and we have to spend the next two to three hours searching for somewhere to kip.

So, I'm pretty knackered today, really. Normally I don't mind sleeping rough too much. You get used to it after a while and car parks are usually warm and dry. But every so often stuff like last night happens, and it really gets you down.

My name's Beth and I was 18 in July. I travel and live with (if you can call it that) my boyfriend Dan. He's 23 and we've been together now for almost a year.

I'm not exactly your average homeless story, but then again, I guess nobody is. I'm from a conventional 2.4 children, middle–class family. My dad's a doctor, and although my mum got a 2.1 degree, she's a professional mum now.

It wasn't even that I was a particularly rebellious child either. I was a straight A student at GCSE level, and pretty much kept my head down as I didn't really get on with many people in my year. I lacked self-confidence, which wasn't helped by the fact that I was bullied quite a bit at school. I wish I'd told someone about it; no one should have to put up with that. For me the easiest option seemed to be to concentrate on my work, keeping a small group of close but inoffensive friends.

I never really thought beyond my exams at the time and when my post–16 option time arose, I was hit by a complete state of indecisiveness and confusion as to what to do next. I finally chose a BTEC in music technology.

The next two months that I stuck the course were to be quite an eye-opener. The people on the course were mostly in their 20s and 30s and they'd lived a bit. They were fathoms above me in their personal development, yet they all wanted to get to know me and accepted me as I was, unlike the idiots I'd gone to school with. My confidence with new people soared and I'd like to think that my maturity did, too. I was now chatting to people the same age as my parents and was getting level–headed answers without being condescended to or patronised.

Being a music tech course, most of my new mates were well into the local music scene. A lot of them were club DJs who were on the dole. They were trying to learn more about the technical side of what they were into. All of them were so enthusiastic about their work and were trying really hard to make something of themselves. I started going out clubbing with them at the weekends and really got into it. It was wicked, the way my work and my pleasure mixed. I felt I was moving forward while my petty ex-school mates were still running around in their cliquey little circles.

However, my parents didn't seem quite as enthusiastic. Being academics, they really wanted me to follow in their footsteps. I began to realise that they'd always envisaged me doing A levels, a degree, and maybe even more. A vocational course wasn't really what they would call education, and although they were relatively OK about it to start with, subtle hints that I should really be doing A levels slowly turned to persistent nagging. After a while I began to doubt whether this course really was best for my long-term plans.

So, I started at a sixth-form college two months into the first term of an A-level course. I was accepted without question after they looked at my GCSE results but was told that I'd have to work my arse off to catch up with the other students. It was a bit of a shock after the more bohemian attitudes of college. Teachers went back to being Mr or Ms and I was treated like a child again, my opinions largely overlooked and disregarded. I felt like I was going backwards, like I was 15 again. It was so frustrating.

I'd chilled out loads at college and my more natural self was slowly emerging. Unfortunately the heads of sixth form saw this as rather too alternative for their traditional attitudes. I was always being harassed and picked on for the smallest of reasons: too much flesh showing, no tattoos allowed, etc., etc... This really didn't help me at all. I'd just thrown myself into maths, biology and chemistry A levels two months behind everyone else. It seemed that no matter how hard I slaved away to catch up, I just wasn't getting anywhere. It was like walking in quicksand, sinking deeper and deeper.

I got very little help from my teachers as I worked to catch up. It felt like somewhere along the line I'd been branded a misfit and although I was getting pretty good grades, I kept being hauled into the head of sixth form's office to be told that I wasn't working hard enough.

After about five months of maximum effort and minimum progress, I quit, feeling deflated and disillusioned with the whole idea.

Over the summer, I took a break in an effort to chill out and have a good long think about what I really wanted to do with my life.

I sampled various nine-to-five jobs to see if any of them took my fancy. Then I got what seemed to be the offer of a lifetime: going out to Africa to nanny for my dad's best mate's kids. I soon discovered the job wasn't all it was cracked up to be. Although the place itself was the most magical experience, my dad's best mate turned out to be less than desirable. I felt betrayed. Something that I'd looked forward to so much let me down with a hefty thud.

My dad's so-called mate turned to me to relieve his sexual tension the very first night I arrived. Vulnerable and confused, hundreds of miles from home, I endured six weeks of the shit, feeling helpless because I was on his turf. The only person I could turn to could have been his wife. As if...

At the time I had terrible premonitions of how the whole situation would blow up if I spilled the beans. Whose side would my parents take: a friend of over 30 years or their daughter? And what could they do anyway at such a distance? All these thoughts meant that I didn't utter a word until about a month after I returned home. Fortunately I got the response I'd prayed for and my parents no longer correspond with Africa.

It wasn't the first time something like that had happened to me. I had a similar one-off experience with a boyfriend at the age of 15. Both incidents have had a long-term effect on me ever since and, although it's not a rare occurrence for teenage girls, it does knock you sideways. On this occasion, as on the last, my confidence took a steep nosedive.

Over the rest of the summer I concentrated hard on having fun, waiting for round II of 'Beth v A levels'.

By the time September came around I was still a bit emotionally wobbly. But, back in a college environment (this time swapping chemistry for psychology) I was ready to have a damn good crack at it. I got along really well and was making good progress as November approached.

It was actually Dan's dog Mac that pulled me the first time we met. It was at a local carnival and I was going out with my best mate's brother at the time. He was younger than me, very doting, and not in the slightest bit sexually threatening. Just what I needed at the time. However, the first time I met Dan, I knew I wanted more. He was new to the area, a traveller, and, as cheesy as it sounds, it was love at first sight.

In my alcohol-induced state, I forgot about the poor

abandoned boyfriend and threw myself at Dan (oh, how subtle and reserved of me!). Despite the negative image my parents and the news had of travellers, I'd always been in awe of their way of life and, for some mad reason, I instantly trusted Dan and poured myself out to him. He was bubbly and bonny, overflowing with confidence. He sold *The Big Issue*, lived in a caravan and was originally from Birmingham (which I knew would go down very badly with my mother!). Blissfully unaware of the future, I was on cloud nine all evening.

The next day Dan and I conveniently crossed paths again whilst on my college lunch break. I managed to have a reasonable conversation with him before scuttling off back to college, safe in the knowledge that he had my phone number. (I later found out that he'd got five phone numbers on the night of the carnival, but fortunately he has taste and chose me!)

The phone call came as promised, raising my schoolgirl excitement to a stupidly high level. Of course, this set off parental interrogation and disapproving 'Hmmhs' were aired as I answered their questions. Trouble was brewing...

Over the next few weeks, Dan and I met in the pub in my lunch-hour and after college. I'd fallen head first and had opened myself up to vulnerable levels, but for some reason I felt totally at ease. He wasn't the slightest bit interested in pushing me sexually: we simply jabbered for hours over pints of Guinness, and it was like we'd never really been apart.

The first time Dan ever met my mum I should have realised it was a bad idea. He was the epitome of all her pet hates: a Brummy, a traveller, unemployed, and a little on the niffy side. Still on a total high of new-found love, I was oblivious to all this and, although Dan was on his best behaviour, I should have noticed my mother's nose turning in an upwardly direction.

Over a shortish space of time, my parents began to fight with me. They wangled devious schemes in an effort to prevent me from being with him. He became less and less welcome in the house, until my parents stated that his dog was no longer allowed on the premises as they found him 'threatening'. That made Dan boycott the house completely, which is what they wanted, but it just meant that I started to spend more and more time away, coming home late and disappearing off for the weekend. Storming rows occurred time and time again as my parents tried to stop me leaving the house, until things came to a head just after Christmas.

Before Christmas I'd been hit by something that had put my emotional balance through the roof. I think it was probably the last straw for me during a very stressful time.

One evening when I got home from college, my parents sat me down in the kitchen and told me they had just received a phone call from my best mate. A very good friend of mine had been on his way back from school on his bike when he'd suddenly had to swerve to avoid a pedestrian. He'd crashed, gone over the handlebars and cracked his head open on the pavement. He'd been taken to intensive care, and about a day later his parents had decided it was best to turn the life-support machine off so that he could rest in peace.

My whole body went numb, jolted invisibly through

to the bone. I didn't even cry, just kept saying 'No, no' under my breath. A void opened up inside me and I felt deadened. Dan was all the comfort I could have wished for, but I was the only one who could sort my head out. The day of the funeral came and suddenly everything that had welled up so intensely inside me burst out in a flood of emotion. Suddenly the death lost its surrealness and hit me very hard. My best friend was wicked; she hugged me and kept me supplied with a constant stream of tissues.

I can never explain everything I feel about it, but it hurt then, it still hurts now, and I guess it always will. One thing's for sure: it made me snap and was probably the reason behind events soon after. Added to the stress from college and at home, it was all driving me up the wall.

The turning point came one night when I rang home from Dan's to say I'd be staying for a few more nights. A huge row erupted and my parents tried to make me come home. It was as if they still thought they had the right to tell me how to live my life. I flipped out and told them I was never coming home.

Contrary to what they expected, this was not just a phase. I started living with Dan in his caravan and got signed up to sell *The Big Issue*. To become a vendor you have to be badged up, which involves being trained and proving that you are in a vulnerable housing situation. You have to pay 40p for each copy of the paper and you get to keep 60p profit from the £1 sale. You are allotted a pitch (you can't just choose anywhere!) and have to abide by certain rules and regulations about wearing an identity badge and not behaving antisocially.

By this time Dan was no longer welcome in my parents' house, which stopped me from visiting home on a regular basis. I tried at times, but rows often erupted and we just didn't see eye to eye in the slightest. I'd effectively moved myself downwards through a class barrier by making this decision. I was selling the *Issue* in the town where I'd been to college and I was constantly bumping into people I knew. The change in people's attitude towards me was enormous. No one knew how to relate to me anymore: they all seemed embarrassed to speak to me and, over time, they seemed to distance themselves from me more and more.

When the weather turned cold, the setbacks of living in a caravan soon became apparent. It was freezing and the cold damaged the structure of the van, letting moisture in, so everything was always damp. Not very pleasant. The weather began to get to me and Dan, and the town we were in seemed grey and dismal. Dan was getting itchy feet again and so, at the end of January, we both decided it was time for a change.

We hitched up to Dan's mum's, where we stayed for a week and she was so welcoming to me, it made me ashamed of my parents' reaction to Dan. I was accepted into the family straight away and was very happy we'd all clicked so well.

Then we hitched back down south to Brighton where Dan had spent time the previous summer. We went to the local *Big Issue* office and there we bumped into one of the people Dan had shared a caravan with the year before. This guy was a right personality and a half. He'd been a traveller for years and, unlike me at the time, didn't take any rubbish from anyone. He always spoke his mind, even if it offended everyone in the vicinity. He just didn't give a shit!

This friend put me and Dan up in the squat he was living in and we started selling *The Big Issue* in a nearby town. I was earning my own money and interacting with all different types of people. Slowly I began to lose my shyness and gain in confidence. But although I was getting better at dealing with new people, Dan's friend was a bit much for me. He was pretty pushy and ordered me around a lot. As he was Dan's mate I decided to put up with it and just ignore it as much as possible.

It was during my stay there that I acquired my first dog, Chaos, the second love of my life after Dan. She's a black and white Staffy/English bull terrier and, as far as I'm concerned, she's the most beautiful dog in the world. She's now eight months old and thriving, but when I got her she was only six weeks, a little velvet bundle that fitted into my cupped hands.

After about a month or so, Dan and I were beginning to get itchy feet again. His friend had left in a rage after rowing with one of the other squatters, and he'd trashed the house in the process. That meant that Dan and I were back to sleeping in car parks again and life was pretty dismal. So we hitched to Portsmouth to visit a friend of Dan's, but when we got there it turned out that the other guy was staying there, too. Talk about bad luck. But, as ever, Dan and his friend got on really well so I didn't say anything.

Between them they decided that we should go travelling as a threesome; first destination Weymouth. We didn't stay there long, though, because Dan's friend seemed to have rows with almost every single person he met, including the police, and we thought it was probably best if we moved on.

Next we travelled to Bournemouth and it was there that things began to turn rather pear-shaped. Dan's friend and I were really not getting on at all. We argued all the time and poor old Dan got the butt of it; both of us complaining and him having to act as mediator.

Things came to a head one night after we'd all had one too many. I'd been fobbed off with the dogs for the evening, and I was stewing. Later that night Dan and his friend popped in to see how the dog-sitting was coming along, accompanied by a mysterious young girl I'd never seen before. I lost it and in a fit of jealousy I started on her.

The rest of the night was a bit of a blur but I knew I'd had heated rows with both Dan and his friend.

I woke up the next morning alone in the squat. No dogs, no Dan, no Dan's friend, just me, my sleeping bag and a bit of money I must have begged up the night before. I remembered that during the row Dan and his friend had said something about going to Wolver-hampton. I ran to the train station only to be told that I'd missed them by 15 minutes.

I felt completely useless. There was no way I could sleep rough there on my own. I hardly knew anyone in Bournemouth and, being a young girl, it was pretty risky.

I rang my mum, not to spill the beans, but to wish my dad a Happy Birthday. Unfortunately I couldn't contain myself and burst into tears down the phone. Mum reacted in the best motherly way possible, immediately offering to pay my train fare back home. Feeling completely lost and bemused, I accepted.

The next week did my head in. It wasn't my parents'

fault, it was just that I had to go back to a lifestyle that was now completely alien to me. Although it was good to relax for a while, I'd changed so much I just didn't fit in anymore and I began to feel very claustrophobic.

Just over a week later, to my shock and somewhat to my relief, I got a phone call from Dan. Mum was livid and shouted 'Hang up!' at me. But secretly I arranged for Dan to call later so that we could talk. It turned out that the friend had done his head in, too. He'd only done a runner from me because our arguing had upset him so much he'd needed time to think. After a week away from me he'd missed me so much he wanted me back. We arranged to meet in Plymouth and I was so happy to see him again. Although it went against every ounce of sense in my body, I just had to meet him and, fortunately, it turned out to be the right move.

I could go on forever about the places we went to on our travels and all the crazy things that have happened to us. I've hitched all over England and I've tried to settle down in loads of different places. But once you're in this situation you have to fight hard to become part of a community again. Dan and I usually end up giving up and moving on.

People definitely look down on the homeless too much without thinking what we they might have been through. We're just normal people who have had some problems in life.

I'm presently based in Brighton and although I'm still sleeping rough, my prospects are looking up. I've got the possibility of housing on the horizon, for me and Dan and both the dogs, as well as endless support from *The Big*

Issue and other groups in the area.

I'm always enthusiastic about the future, and I hope that once I've got somewhere to live I can try to get a job and maybe even get back into education. Whatever happens I'm glad Dan and I have managed to last so long. The two of us and the dogs are a little family. I'm really happy with him and my parents are finally beginning to accept that – hallelujah! I just hope that maybe one day society might begin to accept us, too.

Resources

If you're in crisis and don't have a safe place to stay tonight, you can call any of the following numbers:

ChildLine
For children and young people in trouble or danger.
Call free: 0800 1111

Shelterline
24-hour free national housing helpline: 0808 800 4444

Centrepoint
A charity housing young people at risk, which also produces a leaving home guide.
If you are between 16 and 21: 0171 287 9134
or if you are between 21 and 25: 0171 434 2861

The Big Issue
Gives homeless people the chance to make an income and operates from offices all over the country.
0171 526 3200

Other useful numbers:

National Drugs Helpline
0800 776600

Alcohol Concern
Advice and information service for people concerned about their own drinking or of those close to them. Puts people in touch with their nearest advice agency.
0171 928 7377

Samaritans
If you are in crisis and need to talk to someone.
24-hours a day for the cost of a local call: 0345 909090

Brook
Free confidential advice about sex and contraception for under-25s.
0800 018 5023

FPA (Family Planning Association)
Confidential contraceptive pregnancy and sexual health advice, plus details of local clinics.
Contraceptive education service helpline: 0202 837 4044

Children's Legal Centre
Free and confidential legal advice and information for children and young people.
01206 873820